Bogota!
a Hidden Gem guide to surgical tourism

K. Eckland, ACNP-BC
& Albert Klein, PharmD

Copyright K. Eckland, 2011
Print and E-formats copyrighted 2011
Please respect our work. Our research is solely funded through book sales. If you did not pay for this copy, please do so.
No unauthorized reprints.

Other titles

Hidden Gem series: Cartagena

The Thoracic Surgeons: Bogota, Colombia

Special Thanks

To my family, for the financial and emotional support which made this project possible.

To my dear husband, for not freaking out when I said I was quitting my job to go back to Colombia.

To the various members of my research team, who continue to volunteer their services in this endeavor.

To Mr. and Mrs. Klein, and the Palacios of Bogota for their gracious hospitality.

To Ned Bowden, for buying the very first copy of my first book, reading it and immediately telling me to go out and write another book.

To the doctors and nurses of Bogota for all of their kind cooperation and willingness to share your lives.

To Dr. David Hoffman of Averett University for proofreading this book.

Cover art – clockwise from top:
Panorama of Bogota from Monserrate; Dr. Nestor Sandoval with one of his pediatric patients; Bogota license plate; Anesthesia residents, (Dr. Karen Rossi and Dr. Oscar Silva); valve replacement at Shaio; Dr. Juan Carlos Garzon.

Back Cover:
Operating room at Shaio; Orthopedic surgery with Dr. Cabal; Plastic surgery; Dr. Sanabria with author; Thoracic Surgery with Dr. Mario Lopez at Mederi.

Table of Contents

Disclaimer 7
Foreward 8
Author's Note (K. Eckland) 10
   The Author as the Uninsured Patient 11
Why Medical Tourism? 15
   How common is it? 15
   Medical Tourism versus Surgical Tourism 18
   Medical Tourism in South America? 18
   Is it Safe? 19
   What about health insurance? 21
   Investigative Methods/ Author's Note 22
Travel Basics 24
Before you go: 25
What to bring on your medical trip: Checklist 30
Bogota 34
   Climate 35
   Arrival at El Dorado Airport 35
   Safety and Security in Bogota 36
Hospitals/ Medical Facilities 42
   Clinica Cardio Cien 43
   Clinica Colombia 44
   Clinica de Country 45
   Clinica de Marly 47
   Clinica de la Mujer 47
   Clinica Infantil Colsubsido 48
   Clinica Palermo 50
   Clinica Reina Sofia 50
   Clinica SaludCoop 104 51
   Clinica San Rafael 52

Clinica Shaio 53
Clinica San Pedro Claver, now Mederi 55
Clinica Universitario Teleton 56
Compensar 57
Fundacion Cardioinfantil 57
Fundacion Santa Fe de Bogota 60
Evolution Medical Center 64
Hospital Centro de la Policia 65
Hospital de Kennedy 65
Hospital Militar Central 66
Hospital San Carlos 67
Hospital de San Jose 68
Hospital San Juan de Dios 69
Hospital San Blas 70
Hospital Santa Clara 70
Hospital Simon Bolivar 71
Hospital Universitario San Ignacio 72
Instituto Cardiologia San Rafael 72
National Cancer Institute (Instituto Nacional de 73
Cancerologia E.S.E) 73
Nueva Clinica Los Cedros 74
Santa Barbara Surgical Center 75
Unidad Medica Cecimin 75
Emergencies & General Post – Surgical Care 76
The Emergency System 76
Emergency Medical Treatment 77
Special Emergency Situation: Chest Pain 77
Post – Surgical Problems: 78
Signs of over sedation: 79
Urgent Care / Emergency Departments in Bogota 80

General guidelines for post-operative incision care: 80
Dentistry 82
Selected Surgical Specialties 85
Medical Training and Education in Colombia 85
Bariatric Surgery 90
General Surgery 111
Neurosurgery 126
Orthopedics 139
Plastic Surgery 157
Selected Providers in Other Surgical Specialties 201
Cardiothoracic Surgery 204
Thoracic Surgery 231
References for Additional Information 266
The Surgical Apgar Score 270
Appendix A: Emergency Information / Urgencias 274
Appendix B 276
Appendix C – Limited Drug Guide 279
About the Authors 304

Updates are available at our website:
www.BogotaSurgery.org

Disclaimer

While all of the information provided in this book has been thoroughly researched, this book is not a substitute for medical care or the services of a physician nor is it a recommendation or guarantee of services provided by the individuals listed within. Surgery, by its nature involves risk, and there are no promises or guarantees made with this product. This book should be used to augment other sources of medical and travel information, and, ultimately, should be used in conjunction with the judgment of both the consumer and their practicing medical providers. Health care conditions and facilities can change without warning due to natural disasters, epidemic disease, war or political disturbances. Please be aware of the geopolitical situation of the areas you are planning to visit.

Foreward

Since the last book, *Hidden Gem: a guide to surgical tourism in Cartagena, Colombia*[1], surgical tourism has only continued to grow in popularity. As part of this, as Americans, we have also learned to challenge our assumptions and broaden our horizons. Twenty or even ten years ago, the idea of heading to South America for surgical treatment would have been greeted with skepticism and outright derision. Now, more and more people are open to the idea of medical travel, and have rejected notions of inherent American medical superiority in the face of clear and continuing evidence that this is not the case. This is an important shift in perception, particularly at a time when the American health care system is in a continuing crisis. Impending shortages of surgeons, particularly in my own specialty of cardiothoracic surgery, have made it vitally important that we, as providers, establish relationships with our international colleagues. More importantly, nations like Colombia have encouraged and welcomed our forays into their healthcare systems.

Many of the hospitals and facilities discussed in this book have entered in or are entering international affiliations with American facilities, as part of an effort to ensure that North American patients can feel confident of receiving care comparable to that of home institutions. This has also

---

[1] The most recent revised version is under the title, Cartagena! a hidden gem guide to surgical tourism.

paved the way for increased standardization, according to international recommendations for care, and the accreditation of overseas facilities by internationally recognized organizations like Joint Commission. American healthcare is changing, and it is up to us, as American providers to continue to support our patients by providing safe alternatives for people who may otherwise be unable to seek or afford care. Projects such as this book are part of a continuing effort to provide reliable and accurate information as part of our commitment and care of our patients, wherever they may go for treatment.

Dr. Peter K. Smith, MD
Chief of Cardiothoracic Surgery
Duke University
June 2011

Author's Note (K. Eckland)

This book is more than a guide to surgical tourism. It is also my personal narration of my own medical journey. In this book, I am more than a health care provider and medical observer. I am also a patient. I felt it was important for me to share my experiences with readers, as part of a first person account. Not often do health care providers share their perspectives with the general public, particularly regarding our own medical experiences as consumers. I hope that this book, with both personal experiences and objective clinical data will help the many people out there who find themselves in similar situations. Outside my personal experiences as detailed herein, the information included in this book remains objective and clinically relevant. I received no gifts, payments, gratuities or special favors with any of the parties listing within this book. I have no sponsors or financial benefactors outside of my own family, and thus no ethical or moral ambiguity to any third parties. Any pre-existing or other relationships with persons, facilities or companies mentioned in this book have been fully disclosed. As always, I remain committed to providing readers with accurate and essential information for considering or planning a surgical trip.

It is important to note that this book would not have been possible without the kind cooperation of the local physicians and staff of Bogota facilities. All of these people who welcomed me into their operating rooms did so knowing that they were opening themselves up to criticism, and had little incentive to do so, other than to assist an unknown American nurse in this endeavor. That, I think speaks to the nature and character of the people involved in this project. I must also apologize to the people this book will hurt, but my commitment to the truth remains above all.

The Author as the Uninsured Patient

In the fall of 2010, I was working on the island of St. Thomas in a cardiology practice; after the hectic pace of cardiac surgery, the lulls and shift in focus to long term management was as soothing as the sea breezes and ocean waves outside my apartment at night. But, then suddenly, I fell ill, and as anyone who has been in that position knows, everything changes. Due to poor contract negotiation on my part, I was living without health care. Seems ridiculous, as a healthcare provider, to not be well-covered, and with most positions, it was one of the built in perks. However, at my new position, in a small physician led practice, health insurance wasn't provided. My husband was an independent contract employee, which means he had no benefits either. So, we struggled and finally found an 'internet' policy. My own possible medical crisis was the furthest thing from my mind, until the day I collapsed in the cardiology clinic.

I admit, I had been having horrible abdominal pains the night before, but like many uninsured people, I decided to wait it out. I figured it was my gallbladder, and if I took it easy for a few days, everything would be okay. The pain had eased back overnight, and I proceeded to work. I had already conceded to my husband, that if the pain continued, I would see someone. The pain quickly returned in force at work. I managed to get myself scheduled for some labs, and was scheduling myself for an ultrasound that afternoon, in between seeing patients. I was seeing my last patient that afternoon when I broke out in a cold sweat. I only vaguely remember anything after that, except stumbling out the exam room to ask for help. Very quickly after that, I was seen as an urgent consultation in the gastroenterology office, and then admitted through the emergency room. At this point, the pain was overwhelming and seeping into every pore in my body. I wasn't frightened; I was in too much pain to worry about anything except enduring the pain.

It wasn't until after a stat CT scan, and watching my doctor and the technician exchange glances before paging the radiologist that I became frightened. It's a small hospital, so it doesn't take long to get to know everyone fairly well. There are two radiologists there, a friendly, grandfatherly guy with a graying beard, and the interventionist, who is considerably less warm and fuzzy. In fact, in the past, the exchanges between the interventionist and I had always been less than pleasant; he had an abrupt and dismissive way of speaking with a person, that usually left me shaking my head. It always took a few minutes to recover after speaking with him. It was the interventionist who raced over to view my films. I didn't know it at the time; I was being admitted to the surgical floor, consults were being placed; as any patient can tell you, a lot of things were going on. Most of the time I seemed strangely sleepy, and I would nod off while people were talking to me, and wake to find different doctors at the foot of my bed. It was distinctly disorienting and disconcerting for someone used to being on the other side of things. After four days of a nasogastric tube, and hearing multiple different terms and diagnoses banded about – I was going home. There had even been talk of a feeding tube, but I figured I could face all of that later. As I prepared to go home, the doctor came in to speak with my husband and me. He told us, "There is something very wrong with your spleen. At the very least, it will have to come out, but there is something wrong with your liver too. We can't help you here; you will have to go to the mainland [United States]."

I still wasn't all that worried; after all, it was a small island, and services were limited. I was just relieved to be feeling better, and frustrated about the mounting hospital bills. The next week, as I stood in line to talk to an administrator about making payments, I felt a tap on my shoulder. It was the interventionalist. "Oh, it's good to see you out! You look wonderful," he gushed, sending cold fingers of fear into my heart and chills up my back. He gave me a big, awkward hug before rushing off. Maybe he's just embarrassed, I told myself.

Nevertheless, I detoured to radiology to get a copy of my films. The warm teddy bear radiologist was there, and he sat me down to review the scans and discuss the findings. Then I went home and cried. When I was done crying, I contacted Dr. Hector Pulido[2], and asked for his help. I always knew I was coming back to Colombia, but this wasn't the way I envisioned it. But when I realized that I needed help, I had no hesitation, no qualms or questions, I knew this was the place to find answers. As the plane landed in Bogota, I felt a huge sense of relief. I also knew it was time for another book.

---

[2] I met and interviewed Dr. Pulido as part of my first book in Cartagena, Colombia.

Why Medical Tourism?

Medical tourism has existed for decades but has only recently received greater scrutiny. In the past the United States was the leading destination for medical tourists[3]. However, changing perceptions of the American health care system along with increasing health care costs, and widespread globalization changed the nationalities of both the recipients and providers of medical care. Most patients travelling to the United States for care are seeking advanced technologies (from third world countries) or seek to avoid waiting periods that are endemic in socialist countries. By eliminating geography as the primary determining factor for medical care, our treatment options are increased. Medical care should be about choice, not limitations.

How common is it?

Unfortunately, hard data about the medical tourism industry is scarce, and often from dubious sources. Various estimates of the number of annual patients participating in medical tourism vary widely. Several widely quoted sources cite the figure of "12 million by 2012" but information about how this number was generated is not well explained. In contrast, the McKinsey Quarterly estimates 60,000 – 85,000 in-patients per year in

---

[3] Medical tourism to the United States is generally called "in-bound" tourism. The reasons / rationale behind in-bound and outbound tourism are quite different.

their May 2008 issue[4]. A more reasonable estimate was provided by the Deloitte Center for Health Care Solutions which estimates health related travel to expand to 1.2 million by 2012, with current estimates of 750,000 per year[5].

As health care providers, the authors know first-hand the problems and failings of the current American system. While talks and reforms are being proposed and designed, millions of Americans are going uninsured in the interim. Millions more are underinsured. Even well insured individuals may receive substandard care at American hospitals due to chronic understaffing and defensive medicine practices. Cost does not equal quality in today's healthcare market. The medical tourism industry has now become a viable mechanism to bridge the gap created by inefficient, burdensome and expensive healthcare systems[6].

While popular media and much of the advertising literature primarily promotes medical tourism for cosmetic surgery procedures, millions of Americans are going

---

[4] As mentioned in the report, the figure ignores the large numbers of patients undergoing out-patient or same-day procedures, which represents a large portion of cosmetic, dental and other procedures. This report discusses in-bound and outbound medical tourism. Ehrbeck, T., Guevara, C. & Mango, P. D. (2008, May). Mapping the market for medical travel. *The McKinsey Quarterly*.

[5] Harvard Business Review, The Daily Stat for April 9, 2010

[6] A Gallup poll conducted April 16 – 20th 2009, showed a significant number of Americans were willing to travel overseas for medical care. (Percentages stratified by treatment.) Additional information on this poll available at http://www.gallup.com/poll/118423/americans-considercrossing-borders-medical-care.aspx

overseas for procedures such as joint replacement, bariatric surgery, and cardiac surgery. In many cases, medical tourism is not an extravagance or an unneeded luxury; it's a necessity due to factors discussed above and out of control health care costs. For example, joint replacement costs anywhere from 30,000 to 60,000 (USD) in the United States[7]. For uninsured patients, the entire cost is passed along. For these patients and many others, high co-pays or limited access to health care translates into poorer quality of life due to limited mobility and chronic pain. In comparison, the same surgery can be performed for around $3,000 – 8,000 USD in several countries in Europe, Latin America and Asia[8].

There is no fast, easy or simple solution to the myriad of problems plaguing the current health care system, but medical tourism may help fill a much needed gap. In countries outside the United States, such as Canada and parts of Western Europe, socialized medicine presents its own set of problems and failings. There is no one- size-fit-all approach to addressing these healthcare discrepancies. Medical tourism is not for everyone, and not all medical tourism destinations, clinics or surgical programs are the same. Quality, service, cost, and qualifications of the personnel vary by destination, facility and procedure.

---

[7] Americans consist of 99% of consumers seeking care abroad due to cost considerations according to the McKinsey Quarterly.

[8] While procedure and travel costs are important considerations for the consumer, cost should not be the primary determinant for destination and services. Please take the other factors such as reputation, facility, services, and training into consideration when choosing a medical provider.

Medical Tourism versus Surgical Tourism

Medical tourism is used as a 'catch-all' phrase to describe any and all healthcare travel while surgical tourism is used to more specifically describe travelling for surgical care. Surgical tourism accounts for the vast majority of medical tourism but patients can and do travel for other types of medical care such as chemotherapy and alternative cancer treatments. Surgery, which is episodic, not chronic in nature, more easily lends itself to travel or destination treatment. Most surgical patients undergo the procedure, recuperate in a fairly short period of time, and require little, if any long-term follow up; whereas, medical treatments such as daily medications may require frequent titration and adjuvant monitoring which may make travel more cumbersome. In the literature, medical tourism is the most frequently used terminology to indicate any care undertaken at an outside location, where as this publication deals more specifically with surgical tourism.

Medical Tourism in South America?

Wait! Do those people even have running water? You wouldn't know it from reading some of the outdated tourism literature, but the medical tourism industry has been well established in South America, where specialty surgery, such as cosmetic surgery, is more commonplace. Standards of living in many parts of south and central America rival the United States, with more and more Americans choosing to retire in the southern hemisphere. In Colombia, Bogota is a more popular destination for surgery and boasts a variety of all-inclusive medical tourism companies, clinics and medical facilities, and several well-established programs specifically for international patients. In 2000, the World Health Organization (WHO) ranked Colombia #22 for world health rankings. (In comparison, the United States was ranked #37[9]). In addition, the Colombian government has made medical travel one of its top five priorities for economic growth; to this end the government has been assisting doctors and clinics in their efforts to attract medical tourism, and removing obstacles for medical travelers[10].

Is it Safe?

"Is it safe?" This is the number one question posed by consumers, and deserves ample discussion. The answer depends on who you ask, and what their interests are. The American Medical Association (AMA) and the American medical community have taken the position that surgery performed outside the USA should always be considered an inferior service and places patients in inherent jeopardy. Travel warnings on government websites reinforce this belief. Anecdotal evidence and scare stories abound, of liposuction "gone wrong" with tragic consequences for patients involved.

---

[9] World Health Report, 2000 June 21. Unfortunately, WHO no longer produces rankings, citing the complexity of the task.
[10] http://www.colombiareports.com/travel-in-colombia/105-news/6661-government-promotes-medical-tourism-in-colombia.html
http://www.colombiareports.com/travel-in-colombia/general/12081-colombia-medical-tourism-destination.html. This is just a sampling of recent efforts by the Colombian government to promote medical tourism.

However, medical care by its very nature involves risk in every setting, and it is important to categorize that risk (i.e. is a tummy tuck performed in Rio de Janeiro riskier than the same procedure performed in Atlanta, Georgia or Tyler, Texas?)

Conversely, the medical tourism industry claims that products and procedures offered are not only safe, but often superior in service to American counterparts. A recent poll conducted by the Medical Tourism Association polled patients after undergoing medical procedures overseas. According to their published data, 70% of survey respondents rated their hospital/ medical care as excellent[11]. MTA also reported that an overwhelming 93 % of respondents would recommend international travel for medical care, and 88 % of these patients would use medical tourism for medical care in the future.

In truth, quality and safety is operator dependent, not patient perspective. Patient perspectives are usually based on subjective and variable qualities such as quality of food and customer service. While these measures are important in the overall quality of service, this is a very limited and unreliable indicator of patient safety and patient care. The majority of the most important factors in determining patient safety are not easily discernable by the layperson. These include criterion set by national and international agencies based on years of research, data on infection

---

[11] Survey conducted by the Medical Tourism Association which is an organization created to support the medical tourism agency, which may introduce bias into these results.

control and operating room safety[12]. Some of this information requires on-site inspection for confirmation such as visual and physical tours of the operating rooms in several hospitals in Bogota. For example, the cardiovascular surgery services at Cardioinfantil are standout examples of excellence and mimic the appearance of similar programs across the United States. Surgeries were performed in clean, safe facilities that met all standard criterions for operating room procedures and post-operative care with modern, fully-functioning equipment and state-of-the-art technology. The surgeries themselves were conducted efficiently and in accordance to current recommendations for surgical treatment. These recommendations for the reduction in complications include concrete criterion such as: preoperative antibiotics were administered within one hour of first incision, proper surgical site cleansing, and draping, and maintenance of sterile technique throughout the entire procedure[13]. It is attention to these details, rather than patient amenities, that determines surgical outcomes and, ultimately patient safety.

What about health insurance?

Several American health insurance carriers have begun offering payment for procedures done outside the USA. In fact, some companies offer incentives for their enrollees for

---

[12] This includes the NQIPS, Surgical Apgar scoring and hospital accreditation, and World Health guidelines, which are discussed in more detail within the text.

[13] This is an abridged list.

having procedures done at lower cost facilities outside the United States[14]. If you have insurance, call or contact your insurance carrier and ask about out-of-network providers, and medical tourism recommendations. Several of the hospitals in Bogota have pre-existing arrangements with American health insurance carriers to facilitate payment and patient services.

Investigative Methods/ Author's Note

In a sincere attempt to offer unbiased and factual information on the surgical tourism industry in Bogota, Colombia, the authors have conducted an investigative review of facilities and providers. While we are unable to verify the veracity of all the claims set forth by individuals, clinics and companies here in, we have attempted to personally interview, tour facilities, and observe procedures. Participation by these facilities is voluntary, and refusals to participate or cooperate have been duly noted for your information. However, as part of our commitment to honesty, and transparency during research for this project, the primary investigator has clearly identified herself and purpose during all conversations, on-site visits and other interactions. In the interest of

---

[14] Blue Cross /Blue Shield, WellPoint are some of the health insurance companies interested in medical tourism. Belcher (2008). "WellPoint introduces international medical tourism pilot program: Global Health Care Partnership with Serigraph, Inc. Reduces Costs for Members Undergoing Elective Procedures in India". More information available at company websites. Blue Cross currently covers medical tourism under out-of-network plans/ rates. In several facilities here in Colombia agreements were already in place for American companies, particularly Cigna.

safety and consumer trust, the authors have maintained personal and professional integrity at all times. Using professional status has had a secondary benefit in that it allowed access to facility and staff members that would not otherwise be possible via professional courtesy[15]. Facilities and providers were chosen using both the yellow pages, internet sources, recommendations from locals and referrals from other providers. We started with the providers that were the easiest to find, either by internet advertising or word of mouth. This way we were able to evaluate the services that overseas consumers would be most likely to find. This list is not meant to be all inclusive of all specialties. It is a list primarily of surgical providers and is heavily weighed on providers in the most commonly requested specialties as well as cardiac surgery, the author's background.

Prior to surgical procedures, patient consent for observation was obtained whenever possible.

---

[15] Strict privacy and safety regulations in facilities in the USA and many other countries restrict access to many areas of health care facilities. Few, if any, allow a "stranger off the street" to inspect facilities or interview staff. Use of my credentials established legitimacy in these circumstances.

Travel Basics

The world is becoming a smaller place, and healthcare services are increasingly offered as a commodity as part of a global marketplace. Medical tourism has changed since the days of the Laetrile clinics. In fact, since the publication of the first Hidden Gem book on medical/surgical tourism just last year, Colombia has strengthened its commitment to medical tourism as one of its goals for economic development and increased tourism with the establishment of several agencies to assist in the development of the medical tourism industry[16]. In today's health care marketplace, it is now possible to receive state-of-the-art treatment and care comparable or superior to North American standards at a fraction of the cost with minimal waiting. However, the medical tourism marketplace can be overwhelming, and finding objective information can be difficult, particularly for individuals seeking surgical treatment. In a recent poll, over 70% of medical tourists chose their destination by viewing websites on the internet. As healthcare providers, this is particularly disturbing. The lack of published materials and third party, objective informational sources is problematic and concerning. It was these concerns for both consumer safety and patient advocacy that led to the writing and publication of Hidden Gem: A guide to surgical tourism in Cartagena, Colombia. Since then,

---

[16] These goals were set by former President Uribe, with the current President, Juan Manuel Santos adding his support. ProExport is one of these government agencies.

unverified and unchecked internet advertising for medical tourism has continued, with new websites appearing at a phenomenal rate. Like late night television infomercials masquerading as legitimate programming, there is no way for consumers to judge the veracity of the information provided on-line. This book remains true to the original formula: Information provided in this book was collected through interviews and first hand observation. The participation of all the parties listed within was entirely voluntary and without financial remuneration. The authors have no personal or financial interests in any of the clinics or services discussed within this book.

Before you go:

1. Research the procedure including risks, complications and post-operative recovery times. Make sure you are well informed about the desired procedure, no matter where you plan to have it done. There are several reputable medical websites including WebMD.com, mayoclinic.com.

2. Consider geographic features of the location and travel time as part of the risks and health concerns for the procedure. As mentioned elsewhere in this book, the high altitude of Bogota is not suitable for all individuals. However, the longer travel times involved for trips to Asia, or Eastern Europe contribute to increased risks of significant bodily discomfort after surgery as well as increased risk for life-threatening complications such as pulmonary embolism.

3. **Bring a list of questions to ask your doctor**. You can often email these questions directly to the doctors themselves prior to travel. Be frank and truthful about your medical history and habits. Everything about your medical history is relevant and important. For example, people with a history of radiation have poor wound healing in the irradiated area, even years later. People with certain food allergies are likely to have cross-sensitivities to certain medications. It's not worth risking your health due to embarrassment or shyness. **Be sure to mention if you or any first degree blood relative[17] have had any of the following:**

- Sudden unexplained death (or sudden cardiac death)
- Problems with anesthesia such as difficulty waking up after surgery, or allergic reactions to anesthesia
- Bleeding disorders, or previous reactions to blood transfusions.

4. Plan to spend at least two weeks at your medical tourism destination.

5. Choose your travel companion carefully. **Do not travel alone or bring small children.** Your travel companion needs to be someone who is capable of assisting you after surgery. This person should also be someone who you trust to make decisions for you while you are incapacitated (during and after surgery). While several medical companies offer nursing services as part of the

---

[17] i.e. parents, siblings, children.

package, in general these nursing services are limited to daily visits or phone calls to your hotel room after you are discharged from the medical facility, so your companion needs to be prepared to help you dress, shower, and perform activities of daily living after surgery.

6. Arrange for hometown **follow up** with your primary care provider. Schedule a follow up appointment with your primary provider before you leave, for approximately one to two weeks after your return home. Ask your surgeon for a copy of his surgical report and other medical records to give to your primary doctor. Be aware that your primary care doctor may attempt to discourage you from seeking treatment outside of the local area.

7. While many people prefer to undergo cosmetic procedures with a veil of secrecy, safety is paramount when travelling away from home. **Notify** at least one family member or friend of your departure and return dates, along with hotel information. Alternatively, you can register your travel with the state department at https://travelregistration.state.gov/ibrs/ui/

8. Use caution and good judgment when buying or consuming food, particularly when purchasing from street vendors. Restaurants and grocery stores are safe but the hygienic condition of products sold by numerous street vendors can be questionable. While local fruits are delicious, exotic and inexpensive, wash thoroughly before

consuming. Before dismissing these concerns please consider that the vast majority of transmittable illnesses encountered during travel, including serious or life-threatening illnesses, such as Hepatitis A, occur from fecal contamination of uncooked foods such as unwashed fruit, vegetables, lettuce. This is very similar to numerous serious and potentially fatal food contaminations with E. coli that have occurred in the United States.

This is especially important for all potential surgical patients and in particular, bariatric surgery patients. Surgery itself weakens the body's ability to fight infection as immune system reserves are engaged in healing from the surgery itself. Taking a few extra precautions to prevent contracting a serious food borne illness, when planning to undergo surgery or after a recent surgery, is essential for maintaining comfort, health and well-being. In bariatric patients or patients who have undergone abdominal surgery, forceful vomiting may disrupt surgical sutures. Dehydration and electrolyte imbalances may also occur more readily in bariatric patients who can only consume very small portions following surgery.

9. **Pack light**.
- Travel only with one small, preferably wheeled bag if possible, for your own comfort, convenience and safety. Travel can be tiresome enough even in the best of circumstances. Struggling with excessive baggage can be frustrating when weary and sore. Post surgery restrictions may limit your ability to lift or carry for several weeks to

months after surgery. Don't rely on others to keep track of or carry your luggage.

- Limit yourself to the absolute essentials.

- Bring easily washable clothing in synthetic fabrics such as nylon, or polyester. This will allow you to bring less clothing and wash clothes during your stay. Light fabrics such as polyester dry quickly with a minimum of fuss and no need for ironing.

10. **Talk to your insurance carrier**, if you have one, as well as representatives from the hospital. Many of the hospitals here in Bogota readily accept American insurance. The hospital will help submit your claims.

What to bring on your medical trip: Checklist[18]

[ ] All necessary travel documents (with photocopies of all photo identification) including driver's license and passport. Your passport is very important; keep it handy during your stay in Colombia. This document is used for additional purposes such as credit card purchases, and will be your primary source of identification during your stay.

[ ] Copy of written documentation related to medical procedure, medical facility with local addresses of hotels, medical clinic, and other local contact numbers.

[ ] Copies of all pre-operative testing performed prior to your trip. X-rays and other imaging studies should be copied to CD-ROMs or DVDs for travel. Other medical information can be emailed directly to your surgeon with your preauthorization. Make sure one copy of your medical records travels with you.

[ ] copy of form from Appendix A in this book. Keep this form with you. This will inform medical providers of your medical information in an emergency. Depending on your medical history and scheduled procedure, your surgical team may need you to have some testing before traveling to your destination. You may need to undergo additional blood tests or diagnostic testing after your arrival.

---

[18] Printing of checklist pages, and Appendix A are expressly permitted.

[ ] Current medications along with a typewritten list of medications. Pack medications in carry-on luggage only. Be sure to know the generic names of your medications as these names are the same internationally.
- If you are diabetic, and require insulin or frequent blood glucose testing, be sure to have adequate supplies on hand. Insulin can be packaged in insulated containers to maintain medications at appropriate temperatures. Notify all security screeners at airports that you are carrying insulin and syringes to prevent delays or damage to supplies. While TSA regulations allow diabetics to bring juice, during recent travel, when researching a previous publication, we witnessed juice being taken from a type 1 diabetic wearing an insulin pump during security screening. He also endured several rude, muttered comments from security screeners. The individual reported he had experienced inconsistent rule enforcement at airports, and frequent harassment.

[ ] Support garments as recommended by your surgical team (i.e. sports bras, or girdles). Abdominal binders are helpful to reduce pain with movement following abdominal surgery. Sports bras and other wraps help reduce pain and speed healing after surgery. (Plastic surgery clinics often provide these garments so ask before purchasing.

[ ] Anti-embolic stockings / socks for air travel after surgery[19]17. These are available at pharmacies, medical supply stores, and large chains like Wal-mart. Measure your calves at the widest point for proper fit. Socks should be snug but not painful. Individuals with a history of peripheral arterial disease (PAD), ischemia or other lower extremity conditions should check with their physicians prior to wearing compression socks or hosiery.

- Be sure to inform your surgeon if you have a past medical history of a previous deep vein thrombosis (DVT), "blood clot" or pulmonary embolism (PE), "clot in the lungs." He/She may want to prescribe additional medications to prevent a blood clot on your trip home, particularly if your flight is of long duration.

- Know your own medical history. It is your responsibility to be able to recite important medical details about your previous hospitalizations, illnesses and treatments. This

---

[19] Clarke, M., Hopewell, S., Juszczak, E., Eisenga, A. & Kyeldstrom, M. (2006). Compression stockings for preventing deep vein thrombosis in airline passengers. Cochrane Database Syst Rev. 2006, Apr 19 (2): CD004002.

Philbrick, J. T., Shumate, R., Siadaty, M. S., & Becker, D. M. (2007). Air travel and venous thromboembolism: a systemic review.

GenClarke, M., Hopewell, S., Juszczak, E., Eisenga, A. & Kyeldstrom, M. (2006). Compression stockings for preventing deep vein thrombosis in airline passengers. Cochrane Database Syst Rev. 2006, Apr 19 (2): CD004002.

Philbrick, J. T., Shumate, R., Siadaty, M. S., & Becker, D. M. (2007). Air travel and venous thromboembolism: a systemic review. J. Gen Intern Med. 2007 January 22 (1): 107 – 114. Both of these articles review existing medical data to examine risk factors and prevention of blood clots during air travel.

will help to safeguard your health, as medical records are often fragmented and piecemeal[20].

[ ] Small supply of ibuprofen and acetaminophen for pain and fever post-operatively. Be sure to inform your surgical team of all the medications you are taking. Patients with kidney disease, hypertension or diabetes should limit their ibuprofen consumption. Be cautious using acetaminophen in combination with other medications (acetaminophen is an added ingredient to multiple medications including over the counter cold remedies, and prescription narcotics.) Current medical recommendations limit acetaminophen to less than 4 grams (4,000 milligrams) in a 24 hour period[21].

---

[20] Contrary to popular belief, it's not "all in the chart," and there is no master computer record maintained in cyberspace.

[21] This is equal to eight extra strength acetaminophen tablets. Currently, these recommendations are under consideration for revision, to a lesser threshold of approximately 2.5 grams per 24 hours. Recommendations also vary for patients with a history of liver disease, alcoholism or use of certain medications.

Bogota

Bogota, the capital city of Colombia is a vibrant, sophisticated city. Its metropolitan area is home to over 10 million people[22]. Nestled in the mountains at an altitude of approximately 8600 ft (or 2625 meters), it is a study in contrasts, from modern high rise buildings sharing the skylines with fertile mountain tops and an abundance of wealth evident in the midst of grinding poverty. Historic landmarks dot the landscape of this city, "founded" by Spanish explorers in 1538[23]. There are a few helpful city guides available for travelers to this area and for people desiring more information on this cosmopolitan center of Latin America, which has been nicknamed the "Athens of South America" due to its numerous universities and institutions of higher learning[24]. Of special importance to surgical travelers is the aforementioned altitude[25], which can prove difficult for travelers with pre-existing pulmonary conditions such as emphysema, uncontrolled asthma or other lung diseases/ health conditions requiring oxygen use. People with a previous history of altitude sickness should also use caution when visiting Bogota, and may wish to consider confining their surgical tourism to cities such as Cartagena or Medellin, which are much closer to sea-level but retain excellent surgical facilities.

---

[22] According to data provided by the Colombia government.
[23] Prior to the arrival of the Spaniards, the region was occupied by indigenous peoples.
[24] Please see appendix for additional references and resources
[25] Combined with significant air pollution.

Climate

Bogota's climate is mild year round with little seasonal variation. Spring and Fall months (April – May and September – November) are considered the rainy season with the typical amounts of rainfall doubling in the months of April and October from an average of about 2 inches to 4.5 inches[26]. Generally, temperatures range in the upper sixties and lower seventies during the day, but dip into the forties and fifties in the evenings and overnight. On sunny days, this feels several degrees warmer due to the increased elevation. Be sure to bring along a sweater or jacket for the cooler evening temperatures, and an umbrella for afternoon showers.

Arrival at El Dorado Airport

Arrival at the El Dorado Airport can be an overwhelming experience. The beginning of a memorable journey is made apparent immediately as the Spanish language becomes what is spoken by the overwhelming majority. Going through customs should not be a problem as long as you are not carrying plants, animals, or any other unauthorized items, and you have filled out the customs form to the best of your ability. At the luggage claim area, men wearing uniforms will offer to pick up your bags and carry them out for you. Their services are not complementary. If you are not interested, just let them know. In the distance, you can see the exit. It is an unmistakable sight. Outside the glass windows, a large

---

[26] Climate data courtesy of weather.com

mob of people barricaded from the door wait impatiently trying to identify those who are just arriving. Once you have collected your bags, look for the taxicab service that is partnered with the airport. This service is relatively new and has made a big difference when leaving the airport. You may wish to exchange a small amount of currency before leaving the airport[27]. There is an official stand on the curb that provides a taxicab through this service, making it possible to avoid dealing with the large crowds outside the airport. Make sure you are decisive and you know where you are going next. Request that the taxicab driver provide you proof of his association to the airport taxicab service. Please note that this service will provide you with the taxicab fare price in advance. Once you have left the airport, the rest of your trip should be less stressful unless you are on your way to being operated on, that is.

Safety and Security in Bogota

One of the primary considerations and questions posed by people considering travel to Bogota is personal safety. Recent media articles and travel guides report that Bogota is as safe as any other large city[28]. This is not entirely true and the answer to this concern is two-fold. First and foremost, violent crimes, such as shootings, bombings, and assaults have drastically decreased since the early 1990's

---

[27] Do not exchange all of your money here as the rates are less competitive. A hundred dollars should be sufficient since most hotels and other destinations accept credit cards, and ATMs such as Davienda also exchange currency. Depending on your credit card company charges in Colombia may incur additional fees

[28] http://www.lonelytravel.com/colombia/

when Colombian drug cartels ruined the reputation of this nation due to wide scale warfare against Colombian and international authorities[29]. The most recent data available reports 1,628 murders in Bogota for 2009[30]. In comparison with several cities in the United States: Washington D.C. with a population of almost 600,000 had a murder rate of 23.8 per 100,000 in 2009, while New York City, with a population of over 8 million, recorded a murder rate of only 5.6 per 100,000. Surprisingly to most tourists, my former home of St. Thomas, Virgin Islands reported 50.6 murders per 100,000 in 2009[31], demonstrating that even the most tranquil of locations can be deceiving.

Security in Chapinero neighborhood 1

---

[29] Immigration and Refugee Board of Canada, Colombia: Crime in Bogotá and Cali, activities of the Revolutionary Armed Forces of Colombia (Fuerzas Armadas Revolucionarias de Colombia, FARC) and the National Liberation Army (Ejército de Libéración Nacional, ELN) in those cities, government actions to combat the activities of these groups, and protection offered to victims., 16 April 2009, COL103020.FE, available at: http://www.unhcr.org/refworld/docid/4a7040aac.html [accessed 5 February 2011].

[30] Completed data for 2010 not yet available. Figures from Bogota murder rate drops 0.9%. 16 August 2010, Colombia Reports.com. Available at: http://colombiareports.com/colombia-news/news/11408-bogota-murderrate-drops-09.html [accessed 5 February 5, 2011].

[31] Crime statistics for Washington, D.C, and New York from city-data.com. St. Thomas data obtained from St. Thomas source.com and is gathered based on the entire US Virgin Islands, and its population of 110,000.

Security patrols in Bogota

In response to this, the city of Bogota has established a visible police presence[32]. Multiple divisions of police officers are stationed in the more heavily tourist areas and upscale neighborhoods. The officers appear mature and well-trained in comparison to armed forces often seen in other Latin American countries, and as a visitor, I found their presence comforting, not intimidating[33]. There is also a separate branch of security for public transportation such as the Transmileno bus system.

Above all, however, the truth remains that there is a high level of nonviolent street crimes in Bogota, with purse snatching and petty theft being fairly rampant. The

---

[32] 2500 police patrol to combat spike in crime, 31 Jan 2011, Colombia Reports.
[33] In comparison with previous travels to areas of Mexico (and other areas) where the soldiers appear very young, nervous and unfriendly, creating a sense of unease.

average Bogota resident remains fairly concerned about crime and will state to visitors that their city is unsafe. Restaurants, hotels and personal dwellings are locked after individual entry; many businesses have iron gates and fences. Nightclubs and restaurants, in busy areas, utilize bouncers with hand held metal detectors to discourage crime. This appears to be a norm for much of the city. As stated previously, Bogota, is a beautiful city. And like any other beautiful city, it contains some undesirable areas. Even some of the most prominent and most advanced cities in the world are home to very undesirable areas. If you do not have a valid reason to be in these unfortunate areas, then stay away. Like any other city, it is subdivided according to multiple characteristics such as socio-economic status, commercial vs. residential, etc. Fortunately for visitors, the city's layout is rather straightforward. Calles (street) and Carreras (avenues) make up the city's grid. Calles run north to south and Carreras run east to west, and are numbered, not named. As a general rule of thumb, try to remain between Carrera 5 and 15 (east to west respectively) and between Calles 20 to 150 (south to north respectively) if possible. The aforementioned area will provide a nice reference as to where the nicer/safer parts of the city are located. Obviously, one may need to venture outside of this comfort area. If so, don't panic and follow basic tourist commonsense rules (some suggestions to follow). Depending on where your hotel and hospital of choice are located, you may need to frequent questionable areas. When traveling around the city, try to arrange transportation with your hotel. If this option proves to be too expensive and/or out of your budget, get a map, leave the majority of your valuables in a safe place, and venture into the city with clear plans on where to go and how to get there.

You can always ask reputable people for directions. People from Bogota are busy but kind. They will not mind taking some time out of their busy day to help a lost tourist. Despite the aforementioned concerns, medical and other travelers can easily traverse the city in safety by following these commonsense rules, as one would apply to travelling in any large city:

- Don't walk alone at night, particularly in unfamiliar areas.
- Be aware of your surroundings and your belongings at all times, particularly in crowded areas: buses, public places, busy streets, etc.
- Do not flash large amounts of cash, jewelry, expensive cell phones or other high price items while on the streets.
- Place wallets and valuable personal belongings in front pockets, if possible. Avoid using large backpacks or back pockets to prevent pickpockets particularly in tourist areas.
- Avoid the use of unlicensed taxicabs. These 'gypsy cabs' are no bargain, and are a notorious tourist trap. Licensed cabs use meters and have a number painted on the door which matches the license plate. The driver will prominently display a valid taxi license, usually hanging from the front passenger seat. All licensed taxicabs must display meters in a visible area with an accompanying

reference card that provides rates based on meter readings. Despite these regulations, some drivers find ways to cheat the system to try to make higher profits illegally. To minimize the risk of encountering such problems, try calling taxicab companies when in need of transportation services rather than stopping any vehicle roaming the streets.
- If traveling by public bus, keep your belongings within reach and stay alert. Much of the petty theft occurs in crowded areas.

For the medical tourist travelling with a medical package or medical tourism company, the majority of these concerns have been addressed in advance of your arrival with personal drivers, chaperoned tours, and door to door service to most destinations;, both in and out of the medical center.

Just as there are many wonderful and helpful people in Bogota, there are also many people who live in poverty and will try anything to get ahead. This is why it is imperative that you do not deviate from your travel plans and always be aware of your surroundings. Colombia can be a paradise in many ways, but it has the usual array of socioeconomic problems. If you meet somebody during your travels who is making suggestions that may seem inadequate or mysterious, please exercise caution and stick to your travel plans. Carry a map or ask for directions ahead of time, and you will not only be well oriented, you will thoroughly enjoy your stay in Bogota.

Hospitals/ Medical Facilities

In comparison to many cities and/or countries, international patients seeking top-notch care are generally served at the same institutions as Colombian residents. Hospitals in Bogota are private, for profit entities, with a few exceptions. While multiple small 'boutique' clinics exist, the majority of the private surgical clinics are for same-day procedural based treatments in areas such as dentistry, vision and cosmetic procedures. To avoid confusion, please be aware that the term 'clinica' is applied to both hospital and clinic facilities. Historically, as hospitals were initially established in Bogota, the facilities were specialty-specific[34]. As time passed, most of these hospitals enlarged and expanded their range of services. Several of the facilities in Bogota have created special departments to organize, arrange and assist international patients during their medical travels. These international patient centers assist with travel arrangements, patient appointments, family needs and facilitate the day-to-day interactions for patients from outside Colombia. The centers may also arrange for sightseeing and other tours of Bogota for patients during their stay. For prospective patients who are seeking medical tourism options but are unfamiliar with Colombia, consider choosing a hospital with an International tourism division or using a commercial medical travel service.

---

[34] Such as maternity hospitals, orthopedic hospitals, infectious disease facilities.

All of the larger facilities operate cardiac catheterization labs around the clock, unless otherwise noted below.

Clinica Cardio Cien

**Calle 100 at Transmileno station calle 100
Bogota, Colombia**

This facility recently opened, and was so new at the time of my visit, that there was no website, or telephone directory listing. Taxi drivers were unable to locate it. It is sandwiched in a corner building housing a Davienda bank branch and Sabena travel agency, with poor signage making it even more difficult to locate even for residents familiar with the city.

As a new clinic, the building is very clean and modern appearing. However, the services offered at this clinic are very limited; in fact, there are no operating rooms or surgical services. Hospital floors are small with ten shared rooms on each floor, with only the seventh floor open. The remainder of the floors are undergoing extensive construction. The staff was friendly but appeared young and inexperienced.

During my visits, a patient recounted a disastrous experience at this clinic due to the limited facilities. The patient needed surgery, which is not available at this facility, and waited several days for transfer. The patient was then transferred to a larger affiliated hospital, which is a poor public facility on the outskirts of Bogota. After the patient arrived for surgery and had already received general anesthesia, the procedure was cancelled due to the lack of both an available surgeon and the necessary equipment to perform the procedure. The patient was then transferred back to Clinica Cardio Cien to continue to wait for surgery.

Clinica Colombia

(Also known as Clinica Universitaria Colombia)
**http://portal.colsanitas.com/portal-web/web/clinicacolombia
Calle 22b No. 66 - 46
Bogota, Colombia
PBX 375 9000**
This facility is part of the Colsanitas network. The Colsanitas network does have an international patient program, and the internet portal has an English version aimed at medical tourists, available at: http://www.clinicacolsanitas.com/.

Previous emails to the international center received no response. However, prior to publication, Colsanitas formed a new affiliation with an American company, Sanivisit for medical tourism.
**Sanivisit International LLC
http://www.sanivisit.com
1209 Tottenham Court
Reston, Virginia 20194
(877) 836 3233
monica.wainbarg@sanivisit.com**
During an interview with two of the officers from Sanivisit; Alberto Ospina, President and Monica

Wainbarg, Medical Tourism Advisor, I was impressed by how well they knew the location, facilities, physicians and nearby amenities. However, as a brand new company, there was no opportunity to speak with clients or people who had recently used their services.

Clinica Colombia is large, new, modern and very clean facility. A wide range of procedures are offered including cardiovascular and thoracic surgery. The intensive care units are divided with a separate cardiovascular intensive care unit[35]. There are nine operating rooms in this facility, and surgical equipment is new and fully functional. In the operating rooms, hemodynamic monitoring was noted to be visible from the operating room table, allowing the surgeon to monitor patient vital signs during the procedure. There were no problems noted during multiple visits to this hospital.

Clinica de Country (with signage as San Sebastian del Country[36])
http://www.clinicadelcountry.com/
Carrera 16, No 82 - 45
Bogota, Colombia
Tele: 530-0470
Website in Spanish only.

---

[35] This is preferable to a 'mixed' intensive care unit, with both medical and surgical patients. This decreases infection among surgical patients and allows for increased training and specialization among nursing units.
[36] The San Sebastian del Country signage is on the buildings attached by the walkway, and include the back entrance to the urgent care on Calle 16, and the maternal/ child wards.

It is often referred to as "Clinica Country Club" by Americans living in Bogota for its reputation for serving many of the wealthy, elite Bogotanos. The hospital's name comes from the surrounding neighborhood, called "del Country". Despite being a large hospital, the intensive care section is quite small, with one common intensive care unit of ten beds for both medical and surgical patients. The pediatric and maternal wing of the hospital is in a separate tower with a separate pediatric intensive care unit. The operating rooms are modern, very clean, and well-lit with new and fully functioning equipment. Telemetry/hemodynamic monitoring was visible at the operating table in some of the cases. There were no problems noted during multiple visits.

Dr. Francisco Cabal, MD
International Medical Advisor
Carrera 16 No. 82 – 57, Piso 7
Tele: 530 0470
Email: fcabal@clinicadelcountry.com
Dr. Cabal serves in a dual role as International Medical Advisor for the medical tourism program and as a practicing orthopedic surgeon.

Clinica de Marly
http://www.marly.com.co
Calle 50 #9 -67
Bogota, Colombia
Tele: 343 6600
Email: atncliente@marly.com.co
Website with English language version. Clinica de Marly is a small upscale, attractive facility with just over 100 beds located in the Chapinero neighborhood. This clinic is best known for its DiVinci Robot which is used for urologic and gynecological surgeries. The operating rooms were good sized, clean and equipped with modern equipment.

Clinica de la Mujer
http://www.clinicadelamujer.com.co/
Calle 19 No 91 – 17
Bogotá, Colombia
PBX: 616 1799
Website in Spanish only. The Clinica de la Mujer originally opened in 1989 as a specialty hospital for maternity and gynecology, and is now affiliated with the Clinica del Country. The hospital offers a variety of services as a general hospital including general and specialty surgery along with multiple medicine specialties. However, this hospital does not appear to offer cardiac

catheterization services[37]. The hospital has five operating rooms and offers services in multiple surgical specialties including bariatric, general, orthopedic, plastic, vascular and thoracic surgery along with a pediatric surgery program. **This hospital does not have a cardiac catheterization laboratory, so patients arriving with acute chest pain syndromes have to be transferred to other facilities in Bogota, resulting in a delay in care.**

Diana Marino Peraza
Director of Public Relations & Marketing
Carrera 19C, No 91 – 17, Piso 4
Bogota, Colombia
Tele: 616 1799 ext. 223
Email: dmarino@clinicadelamujer.com.co
Ms. Marino is available to assist potential medical travelers.

Clinica Infantil Colsubsido
http://www.colsubsido.com
Calle 69, Cra 10 A
Bogota, Colombia
Tele: 254 4200[38]
Clinica Infantil Colsubsido is one of three clinics in the Colsubsido empire[39]. "Colsubsido" is named after the

---

[37] Many of the smaller facilities lack catheterization facilities, which are needed in acute coronary syndromes (chest pain syndromes).
[38] The website is difficult to navigate, especially for English speakers, and finding phone numbers proved to be a complicated task.

company that owns it and the neighborhood in Bogota. It operates similarly to Kaiser Permanente and other large PPOs/HMOs. This seven story building was very crowded, noisy during my visit. Very little English was spoken. Signage is in Spanish only. The clinic adjoining the hospital offered multiple specialties including an entire floor for pediatrics and pediatric subspecialties (for example, pediatric endocrinology, pediatric surgery). A wide range of specialties for adults were also represented including neurosurgery, orthopedic surgery, general, maxillo-facial and plastic surgery. The 5th floor is dedicated to dental services, including general, cosmetic, orthodontic and dental surgery. The ophthalmology and optometry clinic was literally bursting at the seams with a long line of patients extending into the hallway. The neurosurgery clinic also contained two specialty clinics, the Down Syndrome Clinic and the Obesity and 'Small Stature[40]" clinic. This particular Colsubsido facility does not have adult cardiac surgery and primarily offers pediatric cardiac services. In fact, **this hospital does not have a cardiac catheterization laboratory, so patients arriving with acute chest pain syndromes have to be transferred to other facilities in Bogota, resulting in a delay in care.**

---

[39] 'Empire' is only a slight exaggeration; Colsubsido is a massive organization that provides a multitude of services; including hospitals, clinics, doctors' offices, supermarkets, banking/ credit services, pharmacies, and technical colleges. As part of its services to its employees, Colsubsido also has affiliations and agreements to help provide low cost housing, discounted travel, life insurance and additional retirement benefits.
[40] Literally, the "Talla Baja" clinic or 'small size'

Clinica Palermo
http://www.clinicapalermo.com.co/
Calle 45 C No 22 – 02
Bogota, Colombia
PBX: 572 7777 Ext. 16031-16032
This facility is located in the Palermo neighborhood. The website is broken. The hospital is a large, older brick structure and appears dated in main hallways but the operating rooms are large, modern, and well-lighted with new, fully functioning equipment. Clinica Palermo is a religious hospital and the head nun is also a licensed nurse.

Clinica Reina Sofia
http://www.clinicacolsanitas.com/
Calle 127, Carrera 21
Bogota, Colombia
PBX: 625 2111
Clinica Reina Sofia is part of the Colsanitas network. This hospital offers a wide variety of services including specialty surgery and has an International Patient Center with an English language website. The hospital is clean, modern and attractive. The ICU is small but appeared appropriately staffed. The hospital, like most in Bogota is completely computerized with computer charting and diagnostic viewing programs such as PAC[41].

---

[41] PACs or PAX is the computerized software system that allows for remote viewing of radiographic images such as chest x-rays and CT scans.

Clinica SaludCoop 104
**Autopisa Norte 104 – 33
Colombia, Bogota
Tele: 653 9000**

Clinica SaludCoop is an EPS (or public facility), smaller than many of its competitors, but it has respectable compliments of services. While the surgeons at this facility do not perform cardiac transplant or pediatric cardiac surgery, they do maintain a separate cardiac surgery intensive care unit overseen by a medical intensivist on the second floor, across the hall from the operating room, along with two nurses for the six bed unit (only five beds in use during my visit.) Hospital has warfarin clinic but no cardiac rehabilitation facility. The cardiac catheterization lab is staffed 24 hours a day by one of two interventional cardiologists[42]. SaludCoop has an International Patient Center to help coordinate medical travel but this department never responded to multiple requests for information.

This software is widely, but not uniformly, used in the United States as well.

[42] In smaller facilities, in some locations it is common for the cardiac cath lab to close on off-hours, which may result in delays in treatment for patients with acute coronary syndromes.

Clinica San Rafael
http://www.clinicasanrafael.com.co
Carrera 8 No 17 – 45 Sur
Bogota, Colombia
PBX 328 2300

Clinica San Rafael is one of the city's oldest hospitals in continuous operation and opened in 1929. It is located in the center of Bogota. This hospital is part of the network of hospitals established by the religious order of San Juan de Dios, (St. John of God). The original brick hospital is across the street from the current, multi-storied hospital building, which was built in the 1960's. While the hospital lacks some of the fancier amenities, such as private patient rooms, the hospital does have a very large neo-natal unit (NICU) and a comprehensive range of medicine and surgical specialties including neurosurgery and cardiac surgery.

The department of Orthopedic Surgery is renown throughout Bogota and Colombia for surgical excellence. There are ten general operating rooms, and four specialty rooms. It is a government facility serving many of the poorer population of Bogota. The building itself is dated, some of the surgical equipment is older, but well-maintained and in good working condition.

Clinica Shaio

www.shaio.com
Diag 115 A No. 70 C – 75
Bogota, Colombia
PBX: 583 8210
Email: info@shaio.com

The Clinica Shaio is a well-known and well respected medical facility in North Bogota. This hospital has a reputation for excellence related to its long standing cardiac surgery program. However, in recent years, this program has been overshadowed by the rapid expansion of the cardiac surgery program at Cardioinfantil, as well as the defection of integral personnel to Cardioinfantil such as Dr. Nestor Sandoval.

As mentioned above, the Clinica Shaio is best known for its cardiac services, but it is a large, full service general hospital and offers a variety of services in medicine and surgical specialties including bariatric, plastic and neurosurgery. In fact, Clinica Shaio boasts gamma knife radiotherapy as part of its neurosurgery services.

Currently Clinica Shaio does not have an International patient program or medical tourism facilitator. Several months ago, on behalf of a patient, I attempted to contact Clinica Shaio for more information for a potential surgical trip. It was a lengthy complicated process, and ultimately required the assistance of an outside entity (a travel company) to negotiate the details[43]. Surgeons at Clinica

---

[43] If you do not receive a reply from either the surgeon or the travel coordinators within 48 – 72 hours (excepting weekends and holidays), plan

Shaio report that a medical tourism program is in discussion but have no additional details or anticipated timeframe.

One of the other significant problems I encountered on several occasions at Clinica Shaio was poor anesthesia coverage. Overall, anesthesia services were a mixed bag at best with patients being cared for by anesthesia resident patients receiving the most consistent and continuous monitoring. Otherwise, the primary anesthesiologist, Dr. Elkin Espinosa was out of the room more than in, delegating anesthesia care to nurses (not CRNAs[44]). Multiple times, the anesthetist would leave the case despite hemodynamic monitors showing significant hypotension, hypoxia or both. This has been the case during multiple visits and multiple anesthesiologists. In some cases this was a blessing, as one of the nurses, Oscar Aguirre, who was noted for his prompt and rapid correction of these situations. My best recommendation to Clinica Shaio would be to consider starting or sending some of their nurses to a formal nurse anesthetist program to rectify this situation, and invest in the nurses that are providing much of the anesthesia currently.

---

to contact another person or facility. Most surgeons will answer in a fairly timely fashion despite having busy surgical schedules. However, in general, providers in Colombia are not as dependent on email and social media during the day.

[44] These nurses were managing the anesthesia in addition to their myriad of duties and responsibilities in the operating room as circulating nurses. The nurses reported no additional anesthesia training or nursing training beyond the standard two year program.

In most instances, the monitors showed vital signs were not visible to the operating surgeons' view, leaving the surgeon uninformed and at the anesthesiologist's discretion. However, this situation makes me extremely leery in recommending Clinica Shaio. A notable exception was Dr. Ivan Santos, who essentially managed every aspect of his patient care in the operating room, including the monitoring on patient status intra-operatively. Cardiac cases are also except from these considerations due to the large amount of resources devoted to these cases (there are usually several residents assisting with anesthesia during these cases.)

Clinica San Pedro Claver, now Mederi
http://www.mederi.com.co/
Calle 139 #94-55
Bogota, Colombia
Tele: 683 9807

The Clinica San Pedro Claver is former social security hospital that was plagued with financial problems until its sale in March 2008. The hospital is now under new management, and operates under a new name[45], Mederi, but caters to the same community of primarily lower income patients. This hospital, along with Clinica San Rafael, and San Juan de Dios (in Cartagena) are all operated by the Saint John of God religious order. This order is dedicated to the care of the mentally ill, and

---

[45] Though the majority of taxi drivers and Bogotanos still refer to it by this name.

established several hospitals in Colombia for this purpose[46].

Mederi is now a full-service hospital with services in multiple areas including multiple surgical specialties; bariatrics, thoracic, general, plastic, neurosurgery, orthopedics, transplant, ophthalmology, ENT, oral-maxillofacial and hand surgery. Mederi has a ten bed cardiac intensive care unit, a 30 bed intensive care unit with a 20 bed step-down unit. Mederi also has a chronic pain and palliative care clinic, and a mother-child unit for premature babies (called the Kangaroo clinic). Despite all these services, Mederi remains very much a busy, crowded teaching hospital. The intensive care unit is mixed medical and surgical and more sophisticated supplies are not always available.

Clinica Universitario Teleton

http://www.clinicauniversitariateleton.com.co/
Autopisa Norte Km 21
La Caro
Chia, Bogota
PBX: 861 7777

While technically Clinica Universitario Teleton is outside of Bogota in the adjoining town of Chia, this small university-affiliated hospital is worth mentioning[47]. While the hospital only has 70 beds, and three small operating

---

[46] The order continues to operate several mental health facilities in Colombia including facilities in Chia, La Ceja, Zipaquiram Manizales, Pasta and Cali.

[47] Teleton is affiliated with the University de la Sabana, located in Chia.

rooms, the physical therapy and associated rehabilitation facilities (including a hydrotherapy pool) are impressive for a hospital of its size. The physical structure appears dated, but all the equipment appeared modern and in good repair.

Compensar

http://www.compensar.com/salud/
Calle 94 No 23 – 43
Bogota, Colombia
PBX: 444 1234

Compensar is recreational facility for subscribers and contains a health spa, fitness center, gourmet food restaurants, self-improvement classes in addition to a small clinic facility and ambulatory surgery center. The Calle 94 facility is a beautiful example of modern architecture with large glass windows and gleaming floors. There are several large operating rooms with new equipment.

Fundacion Cardioinfantil

Calle 163 A No. 13 B – 60
Bogota, Colombia
Tele: 667 2727
www.cardioinfantil.org

Cardioinfantil was founded in 1973, by two brothers, Drs. Camilo and Reinaldo Cabrera Polania, who were dissatisfied with the cardiac services available in Bogota at the time. Dr. Reinaldo Cabrera, a cardiologist remained Director of Cardioinfantil until his death in November

2010[48]. Both he and his brother, Camilo, the current Director, received the order of Boyacá from former President Uribe in July of 2010 in appreciation for their contributions to the health and welfare of Colombians. This is a large 333 bed hospital that is renown primarily for its cardiovascular services but has a wide range of specialties[49]. The hospital campus straddles the intersection and includes an enclosed botanical garden. It has several cafeteria facilities including Dunkin Donuts for patients and families seeking the familiar[50]. The hospital is currently under construction to expand the existing cardiovascular services into a larger, 66 bed building modeled after the Baylor Heart Hospital. A hotel is also in construction within the hospital to house the families of out-of-town patients and the ever-growing International Center.

The Fundacion Cardioinfantil is affiliated with the Cleveland Clinic. This hospital offers a full range of services comparable to large American facilities[51]46 including

transplant, specialty surgery and a cancer treatment center. Notably, this hospital does not offer obstetric

---

[48] (2010). Murio Reinaldo Cabrera Polonia. La Nation. 20, November 2010.

[49] Please look in the section under cardiovascular surgery for further information on these services at Fundacion Cardioinfantil.

[50] However, as a healthcare provider, I must advise moderation in consumption of food items high in concentrated sugars and fats.

[51] Facilities with this footnote offers services that are easily comparable and on the level with large American academic centers such as Duke, Vanderbilt or Cleveland Clinic.

services or radiotherapy. Fundacion Cardioinfantil has several specialty centers including a large pulmonology center for the diagnosis and
treatment of lung and breathing conditions. This clinic includes a sleep lab, and a pulmonary lab for additional pulmonary testing.

The hospital has its own blood bank with an average on site volume of approximately 300 units. English is widely spoken by physicians and medical personnel at the International Center.

International Assistance Center
Institute of Cardiology at the Cardioinfantil Foundation
www.cardiointernacional.org
email:centrocardiointernacional@cardioinfantil.org
Carrera 13B #161 – 85 Piso 4 Torre A
Bogota, Colombia
Telephone + (57 1) 667 2761
Office +(57 1) 667 2727 exts 6404, 6405, 6406, 4301
24 hour phone: +(57 1) 310 680 5298
Website in English.
Director: Claudia Maria Torres

The International Center at the Fundacion Cardioinfantil is well-established and serves approximately 650 patients a year. The majority of these services are cardiac-related but the center will coordinate packages for any condition or treatment as requested. The International Center also offers personalized medical check-ups[52] starting at

---

[52] Also known as Executive physicals.

approximately $900.00 USD including hotel and other travel services in addition to medical services. There is a range of medical check up services offered from consultations with cardiologists, and preventative screenings to more detailed and advanced diagnostic screenings. The hospital maintains a 'VIP' ward for international patients. The rooms are very large, bright and airy with large windows with adjacent sitting rooms for families and visitors.

This hospital is brightly lit, attractive and modern appearing. The medical center is very clean. Everyone encountered during multiple visits were very helpful and polite. This hospital accepts some American insurance plans such as Cigna and Blue Cross.

Fundacion Santa Fe de Bogota
Calle 117 No. 7 – 75
Bogota, Colombia
Tele: 603 0303
www.fsfb.org.co
Website with English version.

This medium sized, 220 bed hospital is the only hospital in Colombia with facility-wide Joint Commission accreditation[53]. The Fundacion Santa Fe has been a member institution of the American Hospital Association since 1995. Fundacion Santa Fe de Bogota also has the distinction of being one of only two facilities in Colombia

---

[53] This is the international branch of Joint Commission, (previously known as JHACO) which accredits American hospitals.

to offer PET CT[54] services, and has a full compliment of diagnostic tools including CT scan, MRI as well as a small separate outpatient radiology center.

The hospital is affiliated with a local university and university medical school, including 14 residency programs, in various medical and surgical specialties, resulting in a wider range of services than generally seen in hospitals of this size[55].

The hospital is planning to become a John Hopkins branded facility in the near future to expand the international patient program. The hospital has also undergone recent expansions in the Emergency department, which has doubled in size, now expending upstairs to meet the needs of the local population[56]. Currently this program is attached to the hospital is a separate building that houses the offices of the specialty physicians for outpatient consultations.

This hospital offers a full range of services comparable to large American facilities. Specialties offered include; general and specialty surgery including transplant[57] as well as a full compliment of medical specialties. There are

---

[54] PET scans or positron emission tomography are primarily used in the diagnosis and staging of cancers. The other PET scanner is located in Medellin.

[55] The residency program recently graduated its first class of physicians.

[56] Fundacion Santa Fe de Bogota had 96,000 Emergency Room visits last year. Hospital staff are very proud to state that this figure reflects a large percentage of patients that would not otherwise have been seen in their facility due to geography or insurance limitations.

[57] Unless patients arrive with donors in tow, organs obtained in Colombia for transplant are allotted to Colombian residents.

several hospital-based interdisciplinary clinics including: an anticoagulation clinic, prostate cancer clinic, diabetes and hypertension clinic, pain clinic and an epilepsy clinic. This hospital maintains 13 operating room suites including new endovascular suites, and is planning for additional expansion. The hospital operating rooms are outstanding; roomy, well-lit with some of the newest technology and instrumentation that I've seen in any facility, Colombia or elsewhere. The endoscopy operating rooms are particularly impressive with four large monitors for intra-operative use[58]. This allows the operating room staff to coordinate care with the physician during all aspects of surgery. The remaining operating rooms have large flat screen displays for computerized radiographic findings for intra-operative viewing. There is a full arrange of patient monitoring devices, state of the art electrocautery, and anesthesia equipment.

They also operate a 24 hour cardiac cath lab for patients with acute coronary syndromes. Dr. Roosevelt Fajardo, who led a tour of the facility reports that door-to-balloon times are significantly less than the current goal of 90 minutes[59]. English is widely spoken by physicians and the personnel of the International Patient Center. The hospital is well lit, attractive, and modern. The hospital itself was

---

[58] This is important; this is the eyes of the surgeon during minimally invasive surgery. Do you really want your surgeon looking through a 13 inch fuzzy monitor?

[59] This is the gold standard for modern heart attack care, to been seen, diagnosed and treated in the cardiac catheterization lab (angioplasty and/or stents) within 90 minutes of the patient's arrival to the hospital. Sadly, many hospitals in the United States can not meet this critical benchmark.

designed by an American architect and is very clean. Everyone I met during multiple visits was exceedingly helpful and polite.

This hospital accepts some American insurance plans. Fundacion Santa Fe de Bogota recently created an international division to help coordinate services and assist international patients. The Director of the program, Ana Maria Gonzales, RN previously worked in the International Center at the Fundacion Cardioinfantil. This program remains in its infancy but is rapidly expanding. This has caused some growing pains; as Ms. Gonzales is frankly overwhelmed with the needs of her extensive patient lists[60]. Another nurse was recently hired but the situation remains less coordinated than desired, with services and calls sometimes returned in a less than timely fashion. However, the staff goes out of their way to welcome international patients; for example; despite her busy caseload, one day when I was with Ms. Gonzales, she took the family of one her patients to lunch to entertain them while the patient was in a therapy session. The majority of the International center staff speaks excellent English and is happy to assist patients with their needs, and readily set up

---

[60] On subsequent visits, after her assistant was trained, things were running smoother and Ms. Gonzalez's patient load was more manageable.

an appointment for one of the members of the research team to see a specialist after an injury during our visit to Bogota[61].

Ms. Ana Maria Gonzalez Rojas, RN
Chief of the International Services Department
Calle 119 No 7- 75
Bogota, Colombia
Tele: 603 0303 ext. 5895
Email: ana.gonzalez@fsfb.org.co

Evolution Medical Center
www.evolution.com.co
Calle 119 No. 11d – 06/18
Bogota, Colombia
Tele: 213 9564
No reply to my inquires for more information or tour of facilities.
This is a private same day surgery center aimed at plastic surgery practices, and patients. Several surgeons are affiliated with this surgery center including Dr. Anthony Salgrado.

---

[61] It is apparently fortunate that the other members of my research team are somewhat accident prone as it provides invaluable first hand material for this book.

Hospital Centro de la Policia
**Calle 26 con 58
Bogota, Colombia
Tele 220 2600**

While security measures are noticeable to foreigners in most locations in Bogota, nowhere is this more evident than at the Police Hospital. Here, cars are checked for bombs with both undercarriage mirrors and police canine units. Entry into the hospital requires passing through security that rivals most airports. However, police and military security were pleasant and helpful throughout this process.

This hospital serves both police personnel and their families.

The hospital is clean, well-lit, and well-staffed. The operating rooms feature modern and specialized equipment such as the four million dollar neurosurgery suite, and neuronavigational technologies. For out-of-town visitors, the main attraction is the seventh floor, which features panoramic views of Bogota.

Hospital de Kennedy

(Also know as Hospital Occidente de Kennedy)
**http://www.hospitaloccidentekennedy.gov.co/
Avenida 1 de Mayo No 75A – 19 Sur
Bogota, Colombia
PBX: 448 0700**

Hospital de Kennedy is a government run facility in southern Bogota[62], which is well known for its services in Thoracic and Vascular trauma. The hospital, which opened in 1984, currently has 282 beds, and boasts a wide range of services including mental health facilities, an intermediate care facility, an HIV/AIDS program, a stereotactic and epilepsy surgery program as well as the complete range of specialty surgery. The hospital itself is dated in appearance, but very clean and well maintained. There are several operating rooms, including separate operating room facilities for obstetrics and eye surgery. The operating rooms vary in size, and contain a mix of new and older equipment, but all equipment was well functioning and appeared well maintained.

There are plans for expansion of both the operating room and patient rooms. Currently patients are housed 'dormitory' style with several patients per room. The emergency department is crowded even during off peak hours, which is unsurprising due to the volume of the population seen at this facility.

Hospital Militar Central

Transversal 3a No 49-00
Bogota, Colombia
Tele: 348 6868
www.hospitalmilitar.gov.co
Website has English version.

---

[62] This hospital is located in a neighborhood considered 'rough' by most Bogotano standards.

This is the main hospital for Colombian military veterans similar to the American Veterans Administration hospital system. The hospital is located on a large campus on a hill overlooking Bogota. The main hospital, a 12 story tower, shares the campus with a medical school and a freestanding diagnostic center. This is a teaching hospital and has served as the training grounds for some of the finest surgeons in the city, if not all of Colombia. The hospital was busy with patients, families and medical students bustling through the hallways.

Hospital San Carlos

(Now Clinica Carlos Lleras Restrepo)
http://www.cucllr.org.co/
Carrera 13 No. 28 – 44 Sur
Bogota, Colombia
PBX: 774 3333
Website in Spanish only.

This hospital in located in south Bogota in the Rafael Uribe neighborhood. The hospital is adjacent to San Carlos Park, and is set back away from the rest of the neighborhood by a long driveway into a park-like setting. This isolation is by design; San Carlos was initially founded in 1848 as a tuberculosis facility. It was partially funded through the estate of one of Colombia's first proclaimed millionaires, Gustavo Restrepo Mejia[63]. The initial hospital design was overseen by an American pulmonologist with all of the

---

[63] Hernandez Alvaro, Mario (1999). "History of San Carlos."

features, including the relative seclusion of the facility, aimed at preventing the spread of tuberculosis and effectively treating the afflicted. This includes large sunlight filled windows, special construction materials aimed at preventing microbes from adhering to nonorganic substances and the trees, themselves, which were believed to have infection fighting properties. Sadly, the original Hospital San Carlos closed in 1994.

In 1995, the building was declared a national landmark. Shortly afterward, the facility re-opened in a limited capacity as Clinica Carlos Lleras Restrepo. Currently, it is best known as the site of sets of a popular Colombian television series, "A Corazon Abierto" which is a direct adaptation of the American series, "Grey's Anatomy." Unfortunately, at the time of my visit I was turned away by security, and I was unable to view the facility more fully.

This facility offers several surgical and medicine specialties to SaludCoop patients in Bogota[64].

Hospital de San Jose

http://www.hospitaldeSanJose.com.co
Calle 10 No. 18 – 75
Bogota, Colombia
PBX: 353 8000

Website with no English version. Email service for hospital non-functional; all emails sent to institutional

---

[64] SaludCoop and E.P.S. refers to a specific tier of insurance coverage for Colombians.

addresses returned as undeliverable. The hospital is located in downtown Bogota. (Note: no visit to this facility).

Hospital San Juan de Dios
Caracas Avenue and Carrera 10
Bogota, Colombia

The Hospital San Juan de Dios, founded in 1723, was once the site of much of Colombia's medical research. However, the hospital was closed in 1999[65]. Since then, there have been several campaigns to re-open this Bogota landmark which was the site of several historic firsts; such as the first surgery in Colombia in 1926 and the development of the first malaria vaccine[66]. Despite being named a national monument in 2002, the mammoth campus, extending over several streets (25 city blocks), is rapidly falling derelict, and in disrepair. While there is a visible presence of security guards, the hospital grounds are rumored to be inhabited by several homeless and displaced persons. Despite the presence of historic architectural structures and an abundant medical history, the hospital grounds are now dangerous, and independent sightseeing is not advised. The city of Bogota department of culture advertises a free monthly tour on the last

---

[65] Caballero, H. F. History of San Juan de Dios hospital. Available at: http://www.pedrocheenlared.es/doc/_fray8.pdf. There is also a locally published book (2000) by the same title.

[66] One of the campaigns to re-open the hospital was in 2008, the '200,000kisses' campaign. Bogota government archive at: http://www.bogota.gov.co/portel/libreria/php/x_frame_detalle.php?id=3620

Sunday of every month, from 10 am until 4 pm. Tours are conducted by former nursing staff of the facility[67].

Hospital San Blas

http://www.hospitalsanblas.gov.co/
Carrera 3 Este No. 16 – 72 Sur
Bogota, Colombia
PBX: 229 1100

Hospital San Blas is a public hospital located in one of the poorer neighborhoods in Bogota. The facility is clean but dated in appearance. The hospital was busy and crowded with patients. During my visit, there were emergency room patients on gurneys in the hallways. Hospital San Blas has an active trauma service, and offers general and some specialty services.

Hospital Santa Clara

http://www.esesantaclara.gov.co/
Carrera 15 No. 0 – 45
Bogota, Colombia
PBX: 328 2828

A former tuberculosis hospital, located in the Hortua neighborhood, this public facility has a dated 1940's - 50's appearance with a campus style layout. I was informed by several physicians that there are no CT scan facilities in this hospital despite recent technological upgrades and the prominent photograph of a CT scanner on the government

---

[67] Unable to verify if tours are still being conducted.

website[68]. Hospital Santa Clara is also the original home and training grounds of Colombia's first Thoracic Surgery program[69], with an average of two to three traumatic chest wounds per week (stabbings, shootings) in addition to the usual complement of thoracic disease endemic in poorer populations.

Despite serious financial constraints, the hospital was clean, and all medical equipment was fully functional and modern. There are four operating rooms, and the majority of surgical equipment appears to be less than five years old, which correlates with the upgrades made by the latest administration. There are still some limitations in the operating rooms; one of the surgeons reported that surgical equipment for that specialty is very limited (with no laparoscopic ports, for example) but that they conserve existing equipment and adapt supplies as needed.

Hospital Simon Bolivar

Calle 165 No 7 - 06
Bogota, Colombia
PBX: 676 7940
http://www.esesimonbolivar.gov.co

---

[68] There has been talk of purchasing a CT scanner for this facility but at the time of my visits, it had yet to be purchased. The doctors I spoke with were unaware of any impending purchases of this magnitude.

[69] For several years, there were two competing training sites: Hospital Santa Clara and the National Cancer Institute. A recent combination of the two programs has allowed for broader range of thoracic disease exposure and experience for thoracic surgery residents.

Hospital Simon Bolivar is a public hospital located on the edge of the Usaquen neighborhood. The hospital is clean, but dated, and crowded during visits.

Hospital Universitario San Ignacio

http://www.husi.org.co
Carrera 7 No. 40 – 62
Bogota, Colombia
PBX: 651 3910

English website available at International Patient Center portal: http://internacionalhusi.org/. This website is surprisingly comprehensive in comparison to nearby facilities. San Ignacio is a teaching hospital attached to the Javeriana campus. In fact, the hospital facility itself is located behind the university library facing Seventh Street. In comparison to many university facilities, San Ignacio appears to be struggling along in many areas, rather than thriving, particularly the surgical specialties.

It does have a small international patient center located on the seventh floor near the cardiac surgery offices. However, when I stopped by, the two secretaries in the office were unable to give me any additional information about the services available.

Instituto Cardiologia San Rafael

http://www.cardiosanrafael.org
Carrera 8A No 17 – 45 Sur
Bogota, Colombia
PBX 328 2300

This is a cardiac services line that offers cardiac surgery at several hospital facilities, including Clinica San Rafael, Mederi and Colsubsido, which is located on the premises of Clinica San Rafael.

National Cancer Institute (Instituto Nacional de Cancerologia E.S.E)

http://www.incancerologia.gov.co/
Calle 1 No. 9 - 85
Bogota, Colombia
PBX: 334 1111
Email: contacenos@cancer.gov.co

Website with English version, currently under construction.

While the sign out front of the hospital is dingy and dated, the facility itself is brand new with more upgrades planned and on-going construction. A physical structure has been built and is awaiting the arrival of a PET scanner, an important diagnostic aid for the treatment of cancer. One of the Directors of the National Cancer Institute informed me that ten percent of all cancer patients are treated at this facility. Unlike the Police Hospital and the Military Hospital, this facility accepts and welcomes international patients, and appointments can be scheduled on-line[70]. The surgical suites are located on the fifth floor

---

[70] This may be difficult for English speaking patients until the completion of the English language portal. If you are interested in the services offered here, contact the surgeons directly.

in one of the new towers. The operating rooms are impressive: large, well-lit, immaculately clean. The rooms are equipped with a full range of new equipment for hemodynamic monitoring and a wide variety of surgical procedures.

Nueva Clinica Los Cedros
**Calle 137 No 19 – 42
Bogota, Colombia
PBX: 520 6533
Email: nuevoclinicaloscedros@hotmail.com**
This clinic is typical of many of the small freestanding clinics specializing in plastic surgery. While the building is fairly new, the surgical equipment is not. The monitors date back to at least the early 1980's, and some of the surgical equipment was much older. However, the equipment was fully functional with recent inspection stickers attesting to this. The clinic consists of two small operating rooms with a 3-bed recovery bay. This facility holds health certifications from the Ministry for Social Protection (as required by law) for procedures in plastic surgery, general anesthesia, hand surgery, maxillofacial surgery, sterile processing and drug dispensary[71].

---

[71] This is important for small clinics and private offices where procedures are performed. These facilities are inspected regularly by a team of six investigators, including two physicians to ensure facilities meet the bare minimum of standards. However, I do not recommend this particular clinic.

Santa Barbara Surgical Center
Transversal 22, No 100 – 24
Bogota, Colombia
PBX: 257 1399

This surgical center is actually the combined offices and four operating suites for Dr. Freddy Pinto, Dr. Alfredo Hoyos and two other plastic surgeons. While the facility is sparkling clean and appears brand new, much of the operating room equipment is dated, but functional.

Unidad Medica Cecimin
http://www.cecimin.com.co/
Carrera 45 N 104 – 76
Bogota, Colombia
PBX 600 2555

Unidad Medica Cecimin is a small ambulatory surgery center primarily serving orthopedic specialties. This facility is clean and modern with three good-sized operating rooms. Equipment is a mix between new and slightly older but fully functional.

Emergencies & General Post – Surgical Care

This is not a substitute for prompt medical attention, particularly in life-threatening situations. This section is here to facilitate the recognition of medical situations requiring prompt medical attention and to aid in seeking emergency assistance.

The Emergency System

In Colombia there is a nationwide emergency assistance line similar to the 9-1-1 system in the United States. To access emergency assistance dial **1 – 2 – 3** from a standard telephone.

If using a cellular telephone, dial *** 1 – 2 – 3**.

In case of Emergency – Call your surgeon!

Seeking emergency medical treatment in a foreign country is always stressful. Add in a possible language barrier and possible surgical complications, and the situation can deteriorate quickly. If you experience any medical problems following a surgical procedure at a private clinic or hospital, **contact your surgeon**. By doing so, you may be able to avoid the emergency room and will be treated by someone familiar with you and your situation. This will expedite your treatment. Your surgeon will also be able to direct you to the best medical facility, if needed, which is convenient to your location and individual situation.

Emergency Medical Treatment

Emergency departments in Bogota, similar to the United States, suffer from problems related to overcrowding such as treatment delays and long waiting times. Some public and private facilities require cash pre-payment prior to providing treatment. Anticipate a request for payment at the time of treatment, and bring cash and credit cards with you. We recommend contacting your surgeon first to avoid these hassles, however, sometimes situations develop that require a trip to the hospital, such as another member of your party becoming ill.

Special Emergency Situation: Chest Pain

If you or anyone in your party has:
Chest pain or pressure, chest tightness, shortness of breath, difficulty breathing, pallor (paleness/ heavy sweating), or other signs and symptoms of a possible heart attack, it is important to go immediately to the hospital for possible urgent cardiac catheterization, if needed. The term for heart attack, "myocardial infarction" is the same in Spanish. Chest pain can also be indicated by using the universal sign of placing a hand over the center of your chest, palm downward. *"Dolor en mi pecho"* means chest pain.

However, at most facilities in Bogota, there are multiple providers available that speak English and will be able to assist you. In a life-threatening emergency such as a possible heart attack, time is of the essence. Delays in treatment can be potentially fatal. Be sure to direct your taxi or transportation to the correct facility, near your location such as Fundacion Santa Fe de Bogota, Fundacion Cardioinfantil, or Clinica Shaio. (All of these facilities are located in the northern section of Bogota and have excellent cardiac catherization lab facilities.)

If you are not near any of these facilities, the majority of other facilities in Bogota have acceptable services for chest pain, with the notable exception of Clinica Colsubsido on Calle 67 – **avoid this facility, as well as some of the smaller clinics listed (Clinica de la Mujer)** as they do not have a cardiac catherization lab, and personnel will have to transfer you to another facility (resulting in a delay in care.)

Reminder: If you are having any kind of serious medical problem, do not eat or drink ANYTHING until you have been seen and evaluated by a doctor. The ONLY exception is for diabetic patients who have performed a fingerstick showing a blood sugar of 60 or less[72].

Post – Surgical Problems:

When you should seek medical attention (after surgery):
- If you develop a fever that does not respond to acetaminophen (after one or two 650 mg doses), **or fever greater than 24 hours in duration.**
- **New/ fresh or profuse bleeding from surgical incisions**.

---

[72] Glucose monitoring is essential prior to assuming hypoglycemia. Even long term diabetics may falsely assume low blood sugar, and treat inappropriately, which may delay the correct treatment. The best treatment for hypoglycemia is milk, not orange juice, or candy, which may cause rebound hypoglycemia within a short period of time after ingestion.

Dark red blood seeping from a dressing is fresh blood. Dark brown drainage, thin watery reddish or pink drainage may be normal, and does not represent new bleeding.

- Increasing swelling / streaking or **purulent drainage** from surgical incisions. (Drainage that is thick, yellow, creamy, toothpaste consistency or foul-smelling). Redness in a new incision (less than 72 hours old) is a sign of inflammation, which is part of healing, not infection.

- **Chest pain/ pressure or shortness of breath, difficulty breathing** (see special situations information on previous page)

- Increased or **uncontrolled pain that develops 24 hours after surgery.**

- **Calf or lower leg swelling, redness or tenderness.** This may be a sign of the development of a blood clot. Do not massage or rub the area, and limit your activity until this has been evaluated by a medical professional[73]

- If your caregiver or family member notices **over sedation, lethargy or confusion.**

Signs of over sedation:

- Inability to rouse, or awaken
- Difficulty or inability to stay awake
- Incoherent or slurred speech

---

[73] This is one of the only times we recommend limited activity after surgery. Conversely, early ambulation (walking) after surgery actually prevents the development of many post-operative problems such as blood clots.

- Respirations of less than 10 breaths per minute (look for chest rise and fall)
- Periods of apnea (long pauses in breathing)

Seek immediate medical attention.

These are general guidelines and are not a substitute for definitive medical care.

Urgent Care / Emergency Departments in Bogota

Numerous small clinics and urgent care centers of varying quality and services are available throughout Bogota, though these clinics are more obvious in the more commercial areas of Bogota where hotels, pharmacies and clinics of all specialties are interspersed with clothing stores and coffee shops.

While we strongly encourage medical tourists to seek any and all care with their established clinician here in Bogota (always see your surgeon first; he can arrange for any other services you need), we understand that extenuating circumstances and situations may occur. If you do need to seek medical attention at an urgent care, bring cash and credit cards since pre-payment is usually required. Bring any medications that you are currently taking, as well as any medical records. Bring a family member to help answer questions and provide medical information.

General guidelines for post-operative incision care:

While each surgeon may have different preferences for postoperative surgical incision care, some general principles apply.

- Keep all incisions clean and dry. Moist or damp skin promotes skin irritation, skin breakdown and bacterial growth.

-In most cases, you can/ and should wash your incisions with mild, gentle soaps (such as Ivory) 24 to 48 hours after being discharged from the medical center or clinic. Pat (not rub) the incision dry, and inspect carefully for signs of wound dehiscence (wound coming apart at the edges). There may be small amounts of clear or bloody drainage. Light yellow (straw colored) drainage that is clear in consistency is a normal finding. If there is no drainage, and the incision is not in an area where it comes into contact with other skin or irritation from clothing, it may heal faster if left uncovered and exposed to air.

- Do not apply any creams or lotions until cleared by your surgeon or until the scabs fall off. Don't pick the scabs, it makes the scars larger. Lotions, even antibacterial ointments, may slow healing, promote skin breakdown or seed infection.

- Do not use harsh soaps or cleansers. Surgical incisions are very clean by nature. Applying hydrogen peroxide, antibacterial soaps or other harsh chemicals can damage healing tissue, and slow the healing process.

- Once the scab has fallen off, (or when cleared by your surgeon), apply SPF 50 sunscreen to your incision daily, and avoid sun exposure to the area, if possible. This will lessen the appearance of the surgical scar.

Dentistry

In compiling this directory of physicians, the evaluation criteria for surgery is well established and easily evaluated. Dentistry, however, is a separate matter and is somewhat subjective. There are numerous dentists in Bogota, and a separate book could be written on dental services alone. Due to these factors, I have included only a selected list of dental services in this volume.
In these cases, the primary evaluation criteria were the collective and personal experiences of others.

Clinica Estetica Dental
www.ced24horas.com
Dr. Juan Carlos Perilla Jimenez
Calle 93 No 19B – 66 Piso 1
Bogota, Colombia
Tele: 481 4348 / 610 32 89/ 800 1885
USA: 305 515 6888
Email: ced24horas@ced24horas.com
Website in Spanish only.
Dr. Perilla speaks some English.
This office is affiliated with Dr. Hincapie's practice across the hall, and offers medical packages utilizing both services. Dr. Perilla offers a full range of dental services including orthodontics, dental implants, cosmetic dentistry (teeth whiting, caps, veneers, etc.) and oral surgery. The office is open 24 hours a day and accepts walk-ins and dental emergencies.

Dr. Perilla's clinic was attractive, modern, brightly lit, and aseptically clean in appearance. Dr. Perilla was very pleasant and knowledgeable.

Dr. Diana Uribe Jimenez
Carrera 16 No. 82 – 74
Consultorio 409
Bogota, Colombia
Email: Diana.uribe22@hotmail.com
Speaks Spanish only.

One of the members of our research team was having some dental problems, and this dentist came highly recommended. Two fillings, a cleaning and a gentle tooth whitening cost about $200.00 total. The patient reported that the procedure was pain-free and needle-free. Dr. Uribe was gentle and kind and performed all the procedures herself, including the cleaning[74].
The office was clean, and well lit.

Unidad de Estetica
http://www.ued.com.co
Dr. Marlon Becerra
Carrera 58 No. 128a – 71
Bogota, Colombia
Tele: 621 7179

Website with English language version. One of my confederates, Gerald road-tested this office for readers. He reported that the office was pleasant and clean. He had

---

[74] The patient did later contact me to say that within four months one of the fillings had deteriorated significantly, and required replacing.

several sessions of tooth whitening. He was very pleased with the service he received.

Vision & Color
www.visionandcolor.com
Dr. Omar Gamboa, DDS, MS
Calle 93B No 17 – 12
Consultorio 305 – 6
Bogota, Colombia
Tele: 610 – 1653
Email: info@visionandcolor.com
Website currently under construction.

Dr. Gamboa trained at Pontificia University Javeriana. He speaks fluent English. Dr. Gamboa is on the embassy providers list, and is very pleasant and professional. He scheduled all appointments without delay.

During the writing of this book, Dr. Gamboa repaired a fractured tooth and replaced several composites. The work was superior to previous work done in my native Virginia, at 25% of the cost. Dr. Gamboa was efficient, and the dental work performed was pain free.

Selected Surgical Specialties

How to make calls in Bogota:
Telephone Prefixes: For land based phones; i.e. Home or office telephones, the prefix when dialing from outside Colombia is 57 (country code) then 1 (Bogota).
When dialing from a local (Colombian) cellular phone to a landline, dial 031.

Addressing people correctly:
In Colombia most people have two last names; the first last name is the paternal (father's name) and the second is the maternal name. In most cases, people are generally known by, and called by, their paternal name only. For example: Dr. Mario Rubiano Smith would be referred to as Dr. Rubiano[75].

Medical Training and Education in Colombia

The main difference in medical training and education in Colombia in comparison to the United States is the lack of a previous undergraduate degree. While American medical schools require an undergraduate degree in biology or anatomy and physiology, as the case may be, in Colombia, students apply directly to medical school after completing high school. Medical school in Colombia is a six-year program, and after completion, physicians

---

[75] Another important phrase in medical terminology is 'medicine doctor' or 'doctor of medicine.' This term is used to distinguish non-surgeons from (doctors of surgery) from internal medicine physicians who prescribe medications, treatments and therapies but do not perform operations.

complete additional residency programs in their desired area of specialization.

There are similar differences in ancillary positions as well. In the operating room, surgical technicians called instrumentador(a)s are used instead of surgical nurses. However, despite this nomenclature, these technicians bear little resemblance to the graduates of the months to single-year programs in the states. The instrumentadoras in Colombia complete a five year training program and can more properly be considered akin to the first assistant role.

Nurses, in general, occupy a different level in the social strata to what many of us are used to; in recent years nursing in the United States has enjoyed a rise in both stature and salary. In Colombia nurses (jefes) and the profession of nursing is often a poorly paid, nonprofessional occupation[76]. Despite this, the nurses I met were well-trained, dedicated, and caring individuals, on par to American expectations.

About this directory

As part of the research for this book, I contacted as many surgeons and other medical providers as possible. I attempted to emulate the methods that readers would use, making first contact via email or websites. As part of my reporting, I have assigned a recommendation rating to surgeons that have been directly observed in the operating

---

[76] This is despite the fact that 'Jefes' or 'chief nurses' as it translates to (RN equivalents) have a four year college degree. Enfermera axillaries are similar to licensed practical nurses (LPNs) in scope of duties and education.

room. I have used standard criteria such as NSQIP and WHO guidelines[77] as the basis for my recommendations. This includes a 'time –out' prior to the initial incision to confirm patient, operation, correct surgical site with pre-operative site marking, timely initiation of prophylactic antibiotics, use of anti-embolic devices, and use of pre-operative medications such as beta-blockers, dependent on specific criteria.

Intra-operative anesthesia procedures were also observed using the following parameters, as well as the application of criteria set forth by the Surgical Apgar Scoring system devised by Gawande, et. al. in 2007[78]:

1. Presence or absence of continuous anesthesia monitoring by anesthesiology or qualified staff. Colombia does not recognize nor train nurses in advanced anesthesia, but anesthesia residents were considered to be members of the anesthesia team. If patients were left for more than two minutes unattended by a member of anesthesia, this was noted.

---

[77] National Surgical Quality Improvement Project, which outlines several procedures to be followed in the operating room to reduce mortality and surgical complications.

[78] This tool is used both to predict surgical outcomes and to quantify the quality of anesthesia using a ten-point scale. This scale has been validated through several large studies involving thousands of patients. Gawande, A. A. et al. An apgar score for surgery. J. Am Coll Surg. 2007, Feb; 204(2): 201-8. More on the surgical Apgar score is detailed in the appendix.

2. Hemodynamic monitoring and correction of significant alterations in vital signs. Anesthetics including conscious sedation can produce significant hypotension[79].
3. Proper patient positioning to prevent injury, pressure sores to tissue and safeguard patient safety, using appropriate positioning devices, and padding as needed. This also included protection of patient airway during repositioning, and during cases using general anesthesia.

Using the surgical Apgar scale, surgeries are assigned a score from zero to ten; with ten being the highest[80].

Surgeries and surgeons were then assigned a recommendation based on these scores, adherence to international protocols and other factors and mentioned in text.

Highly recommended: All standardized protocols and surgical principles maintained, aseptic technique maintained, no obvious deviations from accepted practice. This grading was reserved for surgeons who demonstrated outstanding surgical skills or talents.

---

[79] Hypotension was defined as blood pressure of 80 systolic or below. Sustained hypotension was considered to be greater than 5 minutes, without the use of medications to correct this condition. In some cases, patients were noted to have significant hypotension for the duration of the case, as noted in the text below. Pulse oximetry and oxygenation status within acceptable ranges, or a pulse ox greater than 92%, and bradycardia as defined by the Surgical Apgar Scale.

[80] Further explanation of these scores is described in Appendix A.

Recommended: Aseptic techniques and practices maintained, with minor variations in practice or other deviations as noted in text.

Recommended with reservations: Surgically proficient with errors unrelated to surgical technique itself or surgeon. Deficiencies noted in text.

Not recommended: This may be due to surgical performance, failure to follow standardized protocols or other factors as noted in text.

Bariatric Surgery

Contrary to popular belief, gastric bypass surgery and other bariatric surgeries are not "the easy way" to lose weight. These procedures are life-saving for obese patients, particularly those suffering from obesity related conditions such as diabetes, cardiac conditions, and degenerative joint disease. Unfortunately, in North American society, judgmental attitudes from the general public and providers alike often make the decision to pursue surgery more difficult. Despite a wide body of medical literature supporting bariatric surgery, particularly gastric bypass surgery for obesity, the American Heart Association recently released a statement recommending surgery only "as a last resort for morbidly obese," and strongly encouraging less effective surgical techniques such as gastric banding. While surgery is never to be taken lightly, this attitude hinders care of these patients. This is in contrast to international attitudes regarding the treatment of obesity and diabetes, as expressed by the International Diabetes Federation (IDF) who recently (May 2011) recommended early gastric bypass surgery in obese patients with diabetes as part of an aggressive strategy to prevent the development of diabetic complications such as vision loss, limb loss and cardiovascular disease (heart attacks.)

Like any surgical procedure, bariatric procedures carry significant risk of complications, but for many people this risk is trivial in comparison to existing or developing obesity –related problems. There are several international

guidelines related to performing bariatric procedures, specifically gastric bypass, which is the most drastic (and effective) procedure when compared to gastric balloon or sleeve gastrectomy. The criteria for bariatric surgery are based on BMI (Body Mass Index[81]). Surgical guidelines currently state that surgery is indicated when:
- BMI is 35 or greater and patient has an obesity related condition (diabetes, hypercholesteremia, and hypertension).
- BMI of 40 or greater.

Gastric bypass (Roux- en- Y) is also the procedure of choice to treat diabetes. Research has shown gastric bypass surgery to be an effective treatment at eliminating diabetes[82]. Within 48 hours of surgery, the majority of patients' glucose has returned to normal, and these patients will no longer require oral or injectable medications. Newer international guidelines to address the treatment of diabetes in patients that otherwise fail to meet the criteria have not yet been developed[83]. However there are some experimental protocols aimed at treating these individuals.

Treatment of obesity requires a multi-disciplinary approach, in addition to surgery for optimal results including diet/ nutritional counseling, physical therapy

---

[81] There are numerous BMI calculators available on-line. One of my favorites is the West Virginia Dietetic Website at www.wvda.org. The site also has activity calculators and dietary information

[82] This is most effective in patients who have had diabetes for eight years or less.

[83] An example: Patient with uncontrolled diabetes and a BMI of 32.

and psychological counseling. Psychological evaluation is particularly important during the post-operative period to identify food triggers and other components of maladaptive eating behaviors, which may otherwise lead to self-destructive behaviors and subsequent weight gain[84]. Gastric bypass procedures used to involve a large abdominal incision, but are now usually done endoscopically with several very small incisions (ports). This means that risk of infection is decreased, mobility and recovery time is accelerated and overall morbidity is decreased.

Surprisingly, the majority of surgeons specializing in bariatric surgery are not well advertized on the internet or in more conventional media[85].

Cirugia Bariatrica y Metabolica
http://www.cirugiaparalaobesidad.com/
Carrera 14 No 127 – 11
Consultorio 408
Bogota, Colombia
Tele: 658 1604
Email: drmikler@yahoo.com

Dr. Mikler initially appeared on the Association for Obesity and Bariatric Surgery member listing. While he is on the internet, his website does not appear in

---

[84] The causes of obesity are multi-factorial and more complex than excessive calorie intake. There are sociological (cultural), psychological and biological components to obesity.

[85] There are only three listings in the phonebook for bariatric surgeons, and a conventional internet search gives limited results as well

conventional English language searches. He replied quickly to an email requesting a meeting. Dr. Mikler notified me the morning of our meeting that he might be delayed and thoughtfully rescheduled the meeting to a convenient location, later in the day.

Website in Spanish only. (Please note that while this website address is very similar to the clinic below, these are two separate practices.) Dr. Mikler speaks good but not fluent English.

Dr. Mikler is the President of the Colombian Association of Obesity and Bariatric Surgery, and is the President of the 2011 Latin American conference of the International Federation of Surgery for Obesity as well as a member of several other organizations including the Colombian Surgical Association[86]. Since Dr. Mikler began performing bariatric procedures in 1997, he has performed over 2500 surgeries[87].

There are several other physicians within Dr. Mikler's practice, and he reports that he is always assisted by a second surgeon in the operating room.

Dr. Mikler operates at several hospitals including Clinica Palermo, Clinica de la Mujer, Clinica Marly and Clinica del Country. He currently performs 10 surgeries per week, 1 - 2 per day. He states he previously performed 4 -5

---

[86] Dr. Mikler is also a member of the following: American Society of Metabolic and Bariatric Surgery, International Surgical Association, Latin American Association of Endoscopic Surgery, Colombian Association of Clinical Nutrition, Colombian Society of the Management of Obesity and the Ecuadorian Society of Bariatric Surgery.

[87] As of 2010.

surgeries per day, but he enjoys having more time to spend with his patients. He is friendly and affable; his silver hair belies his boyish charm.

He offers medical tourism packages[88] for out-of-town patients and has operated on around 150 North American patients at the time of our initial interview. During a case with Dr. Mikler, at Clinica Palermo, he was assisted by two other surgeons: Dr. Eduardo Silva, and Dr. Diana Gomez. The patient received sedation and anesthesia after the surgeon entered the room, in his presence. The anesthesiologist, Dr. Rincon, stayed in the room and directly observed the patient during the entire case. The staff used electronic charting software, and followed all standardized protocols; patient was appropriately identified, marked and antibiotics administered in a timely fashion. Proper patient draping and positioning was performed by Dr. Mikler and his staff[89]. Pneumatic compression devices were applied prior to sterile preparations[90]. All equipment was modern and well maintained. Nursing staff was able to anticipate the physician's needs.

Surgical Apgar score for case: 9

---

[88] Prices vary with procedure and patient, but he quoted around $9500 for surgery alone and $13,000 for a full package.

[89] This is important to prevent the development of pressure sores "bedsores," deep vein thrombosis and other soft tissue injuries during surgery. These pressure sores can occur in just a few hours without proper precautions.

[90] To prevent deep vein thrombosis, most surgeons use either pneumatic compression devices or ted hose.

Highly recommended, personal attention to details by surgeon.

Dr. Eduardo Silva Bermudez, MD
http://www.vivirinobesidad.com
Calle 91 No 19 C – 55
Consultorio 409
Bogota, Colombia
Tele: 691 0647
Email: edo_silva@yahoo.com
Dr. Silva is a bariatric surgeon, who works with Dr. Mikler. I initially met Dr. Silva in the operating room with Dr. Mikler. Dr. Silva speaks Spanish only. Dr. Silva is proficient and skilled in the operating room.
Recommended.

Dr. Amalia Anaya, MD
Dr. Anaya is a medical internist specializing in the medical treatment of obesity[91]. She also performs pre-operative evaluation of patients.
Dr. Ma Cecilia Vallejo is the psychiatrist within Dr. Mikler's practice.

---

[91] "Medical treatment" or "medical management" are terms used to denote all nonsurgical treatments of diseases or conditions; i.e. medicines, therapies.

Cirugía Para La Obesidad
http://www.cirugiaparalaobesidad.com.co/
Calle 83 No. 16A 11
Bogotá, Colombia
PBX: 5302875 / 6919557
Email: contactus@cirugiaparalaobesidad.com.co

Dr. Chaux called within minutes of receiving my message and set up a meeting that afternoon. While the office staff have limited to no English, Dr. Chaux and several of the other physicians are fluent in English. The clinic occupies a freestanding building located behind Clinica del Country. The building is new appearing, clean, well lit, and decorated attractively. There are several computers in the lobby for patient use. There is also a flat screen television which broadcasts information about the surgical procedures[92].

This group is composed of several of the surgeons profiled with Dr. Francisco Holguin in Cartagena. This group consists of five surgeons; Dr. Chaux, Dr. Franco, Dr. Fortero and Dr. Botanos[93] who primarily operate in Bogota but also operate in Cartagena, and other cities in Colombia. They are all members of the Colombian Surgical Association.

The Bogota clinic performs approximately twenty procedures per week at the Clinica del Country hospital. The average hospital stay for patients undergoing gastric

---

[92] I viewed the patient information programs (in Spanish), which are refreshingly straight forward. Risks of surgery and the drastic nature of the procedure and post-operative lifestyles are discussed in a frank manner.
[93] In addition to Dr. Holguin, who primarily operates in Cartagena.

bypass is two days, with one day on average for gastric sleeve procedures.

Dr. Carlos Felipe Chaux Mosquera

Dr. Chaux has been performing laparoscopic surgery for over 18 years dedicating the last ten years primarily to bariatric surgery. Prior to this, he was a trauma surgeon in his hometown of Popayan, Colombia. He is an experienced general surgeon with specialty foci in the areas of pancreatic, biliary, splenic, and colon surgery[94]. He also has experience in thoracic surgery including paraesophageal surgery[95].

Currently he maintains busy practices in Bogota and Cali. He operates in the Bogota clinic on Mondays, Tuesdays and Wednesdays. The remainder of the week is spent travelling and operating in several areas throughout Colombia: Cali, Cartagena, Popayan, Monterrey, Cocora, and Naba. He also mentors surgeons from all over South America, who often observe in the clinic and the operating room. There is some criticism of Dr. Chaux by other local surgeons due to his frequent travel; more than one surgeon complained that he "gets stuck treating his complications". However, I was unable to confirm the veracity of this statement or the frequency of post-operative complications, and as one of the more prominent surgeons in his field, it is possible that this claim was made for reasons other than as stated.

---

[94] There is no bariatric surgery specialty certification or credential.

[95] Dr. Chaux is not a specialty trained thoracic surgeon.

Dr. Chaux operates primarily on adults but also operates on morbidly obese adolescents. He stresses that the pre-surgical psychological counseling is particularly important for adolescent and young adult patients. Dr. Chaux also discusses the effectiveness of these procedures, recommending endoscopic balloon as an adjunctive treatment to diet and exercise for the moderately overweight only[96]. After spending several hours in the operating room with Dr. Chaux, observing several surgical procedures, I am very pleased with the surgical staff, equipment and facilities available at Clinica del Country. I am also very comfortable with Dr. Chaux and his surgical habits; he has a meticulous attention to detail and requires precision and synchronization from his staff . Sterility was maintained throughout the cases, with patients properly draped and positioned. All standard protocols were followed.

Apgar scores: 9, consistently
Highly recommended.

Dr. Francisco Holguin Rueda, MD, FACS

As mentioned above, Dr. Holguin was previously profiled in the Cartagena book, and like Dr. Chaux and the rest of the practice, operates at several different facilities. He currently divides his time between Bogota and Cartagena. He is fluent in English.

---

[96] Not an effective treatment for morbid obesity. Gastric bypass surgery is the treatment of choice for obese patients, and patients with metabolic disorders (diabetes). Gastric sleeve is significantly less effective in this population and carries an increased risk of complications

Dr. Holguin is a former trauma surgeon who now specializes in Bariatric surgery. He attended medical school at Javeriana, and completed his general surgery residency at the University of Connecticut, and a trauma fellowship at Shock Trauma, in Baltimore, Maryland, with the University of Maryland. He has additional training in laparoscopic surgery. He is board certified with the American Board of Surgeons and is a former fellow in the American College of Surgeons.

Dr. Holguin no longer operates the Medi-help clinic in Cartagena but is involved in a new project, "Medical City," which is a large multi-specialty hospital complex to be built right outside of Cartagena. Groundbreaking is to take place sometime in 2012.

Ms. Claudia Fresneda Plazas, RN is the clinic coordinator for international patients. Ms. Fresneda and the nutritionist also speak excellent English. The nutritionist provided me with a detailed explanation of the nutrition services provided to patients along with a copy of the meal plans. Patients meet with the nutritionist several times, pre and post operatively, to discuss critical dietary changes after surgery. She performs monthly check ups with weigh-ins for local patients and remote services for international patients[97].

---

[97] Monthly post-operative nutritionist sessions for a minimum of one year, longer as needed.

Dr. Camilo Diaz Rincon
www.bypassgastrico.com
Carrera 16 No. 82 – 51
Consultorio 301
Bogota, Colombia
Email: camilodiazmd@hotmail.com
Attempted to contact Dr. Diaz. No reply received.
Website in Spanish only.
Dr. Diaz has been performing bariatric procedures since 1999, and has performed over 1400 operations, according to his website.
Member of multiple surgical societies: Colombian Surgical Association, Colombian Association for Obesity & Bariatric Surgery, International Society of Surgery, and the International Federation for Surgery and Obesity.

Grammo
www.gramma.org
Director: Dr. Cesar Guevara, MD
Clinica Shaio
Diag 115 A No. 70 C – 75
Casa 4, Piso 1
Bogota, Colombia
Tele: 271 6531

Carrera 116 No. 82 – 74
Consultorio 504
Edificio San Sebastian del Country
Tele: 271 6539
Email: info@grammo.org

Emailed with follow up visit in person. Dr. Guevara was not available to speak with me, but left a written message with his staff. Dr. Guevara followed up with a phone call to schedule a visit to his clinic.

Website with English language version. Grammo is a large multi-disciplinary bariatric clinic with several bariatric surgeons. Dr. Cesar Ernesto Guevara Perez is the director of Grammo and the coordinator of the bariatric surgery program at the Shaio Clinic. He is the Vice President of the Colombian Association of Obesity and Bariatric Surgery. He also serves on the executive committee for the most recent Latin American conference as secretary of the International Federation for Obesity Surgery[98]. He is a member of the Colombian Surgical Association. Dr. Guevara speaks limited English. He is a very pleasant, young appearing surgeon who is happy to accommodate my requests, and answer questions. In his spare time, Dr. Guevara plays chess, and enjoys watching football and soccer.

Currently he is joined by two other bariatric surgeons at Clinica Shaio, the father and son team of Dr. Ruben Francisco Luna Romero and Dr. Ruben Daniel Luna Alvarez.

Dr. Guevara has worked with Clinica Shaio for over ten years and added Clinica del Country to his practice three years ago.

---

[98] At the time of my initial visit, he was preparing for the Latin American Congress on Obesity and Obesity Surgery along with several other members profiled here.

He is joined at Clinica del Country by another surgeon. Dr. Guevara's wife also works as a scrub nurse in the operating room at Clinica de Country.

His practice, Grammo, also provides multi-disciplinary care including a nutritionist, a physical therapist and a psychologist.

Currently there is no international patient program or services specifically aimed at assisting medical tourists at Clinica Shaio, but Clinica del Country does have an international patient program.

Dr. Ruben Francisco Luna Romero, MD is also the Chief of Surgery at the Shaio Clinic. Both Dr. Lunas are members of the Colombian Association for Obesity and Bariatric Surgery. Dr. Luna is a general and transplant surgeon[99]. He reports that he was initially training to be an engineer and had entered his third year of study in Spain when he decided to switch to medicine. He stated he had initially been dissuaded from medicine due to the long hours he saw his father work as a general surgeon. Dr. Luna attended Universitario del Rosario for both medical school and his general surgery residency. He was working at San Rafael Hospital when he was approached by his department head, who encouraged further specialization. At that time, Dr. Luna's sister was the Heart - Lung Transplant Coordinator at the University of Minnesota[100], and she helped arrange for Dr. Luna to complete a

---

[99] Renal (kidney) and pancreatic transplant.

[100] She is now retired.

transplant fellowship under the guidance of Dr. David Sutherland[101]. After his return to Colombia, Dr. Luna performed the first kidney transplant at Clinica San Rafael on Oct. 31, 1985[102]. He went on to perform the first kidney / pancreas transplant at San Pedro Claver in 1987, and was part of the team performing the first heart – kidney transplant at Clinica Shaio in 1997. He started a foundation to support organ transplantation for children and performed over sixty transplants[103]. His organization also convinced several drug companies to provide anti-rejection medications to the children for free. Dr. Luna helped to establish transplant surgery programs at Clinica Shaio, Colsubsido, San Pedro Claver and Clinica San Rafael. In 1991 he was named the Outstanding Young Person of the World for medical innovation[104]. He also established the regional procurement program now in place in Bogota.

However, all of these achievements have taken their toll; at 36, Dr. Luna had his first heart attack. Despite two subsequent heart attacks and cardiac surgery, Dr. Luna continues to maintain a full-time surgical practice. In his spare time, he has recently taken up golf.

---

[101] Dr. David Sutherland is widely acknowledged as one of the pioneers in organ transplantation.

[102] This was not the first kidney transplant in Colombia, which dates back to the 1960's, at Hospital San Juan de Dios.

[103] For free, as part of his charitable foundation.

[104] This recognition is provided by the Junior Chamber International (JCI). More about this organization can be found on their homepage at www.jci.cc

Dr. Ruben Daniel Luna Alvaro, MD is a third generation general surgeon and maintains an active general surgery practice in addition to performing bariatric surgery and kidney transplantation as a staff physician at Clinica Shaio. He has been operating since 2005. He attended medical school at National University and completed his general surgery residency at El Bosque. He completed a three-month visiting fellowship at the University of Minnesota. He traveled to San Pablo for a short course in bariatric surgery and reports that he currently performs about 2 – 3 bariatric procedures per week. Kidney transplants are more sporadic in nature, and he estimates that he performs about 35 per year, and has completed over 80 to date. The majority of these transplant surgeries have used cadaver kidneys, but he does perform living –related transplantation. For medical travelers, he cautions that the organ recipient would have to be in Bogota for approximately one month, and would need to have a nephrologist with transplant training to follow the patient, back in their city of origin. The organ donor would require a 10 – 15 day stay post-surgery for recuperation before returning home.

In his spare time, he enjoys playing soccer, watching movies, traveling and spending time with his family[105]. In the operating room, all preoperative protocols and procedures are followed. Patient positioning and application of anti-embolic devices are performed by Dr. Luna.

---

[105] His wife, Dr. Andrea Oviedo is in family practice.

Anesthesia was managed by Dr. Espinosa, with frequent, uncorrected episodes of hypotension, significant bradycardia and the absence of continuous monitoring. At one point during the case, the anesthesiologist left the room[106], while hemodynamic monitoring showed a blood pressure (by cuff) of 66/46. No attempts were made during any of the hypotensive episodes to verify readings or adjust the cuff to ensure accuracy. The monitor showing vital signs was turned out of the surgeon's line of vision, and the alarms were turned down to low levels[107]. Dr. Luna follows a two-surgeon policy and was assisted by Dr. Cesar Guevara during the case. The necessity of this policy became evident when in mid-surgery, Dr. Luna stepped out of the room to visit another operating room for a few minutes, and Dr. Guevara had to assume control of the surgery. The surgical procedure itself went well. Notably, while the majority of bariatric surgeons reinforce the staple line by over sewing[108], Dr. Luna did not.

Surgical Apgar score: 4

Not recommended due to the quality of anesthesia.

---

[106] At 9:25 am, during the surgery, Dr. Espinosa left the operating room, and did not return, the case concluded at 9:53 am.

[107] Standing just behind the surgeon and to the left (out of the surgical sterile field), only the black plastic back of the monitor was visible, and the telemetry was faintly audible over the other sounds of the room.

[108] This is done to prevent dehiscence of the sutures with spillage of gastric contents because the new, smaller stomach (and the suture line) is under increased pressure due to its decreased capacity.

Dr. Diana Cristina Gomez Malo, MD
http://www.dragomez-bypassgastrico.com/
Ave Cra 19 No 95 – 55
Consultorio 310
Bogota, Colombia
Email: dianacristinagomezmalo@hotmail.com

Emailed to request interview. Dr. Gomez answered my emails promptly to schedule an interview. Our initial meeting preceded our scheduled interview, Dr. Gomez assisted in one of Dr. Mikler's cases. Dr. Gomez primarily speaks Spanish.

Dr. Gomez is a bariatric surgeon and coordinator of this practice, which contains several specialties including bariatric surgery, general surgery, plastic surgery along with ancillary services such as psychiatry and nutrition. Dr. Gomez is a member of the Colombian Society for Obesity and Bariatric Surgery, and her contact information was obtained through that organization.

She is also a member of the Colombia Surgical Association, Colombian Foundation of the Management of Obesity, and the Colombian Medical College. Dr. Gomez also works with Dr. Rami Mikler, as mentioned above.

In her spare time she is learning Italian.

In the operating room she was competent, skilled and proficient.

Highly recommended.

Dr. Gabriel Alberto Roa Rossi, MD

Dr. Roa is another bariatric surgeon associated with Dr.

Gomez's practice. He is a member of multiple organizations including Colombian Surgical Association, Colombian Trauma Association, Latin American Endoscopic Surgery Association and the PanAmerican Trauma Society.

Dr. German Prieto Sanchez, MD
Dr. Prieto is a general surgeon specializing in gastroenterology. He is a member of the Colombian Surgical Association, and the Colombian Trauma Society.

Dr. Claudia Patricia Nieto Gonzales, MD
Dr. Nieto is a plastic surgeon in Dr. Gomez' practice. She is a member of the Colombian Surgical Association, Latin American Federation of Plastic Surgery and the International Confederation for Plastic and Reconstructive Surgery.

Dr. Ricardo Manuel Nasser Bechara
http://www.ricardonassarmd.com/
Fundacion Santa Fe de Bogota
Ave 9 No. 117-20
Consultorio 613
Bogota, Colombia
Tele: 215 – 0375
Email: multiple addresses:
rnassarmd@yahoo.com
rnassarmd@gmail.com
rnassarmd@hotmail.com
rnassar@fundacionsantafe.com

Website with English version.

Dr. Nasser speaks English, French and Spanish.

Dr. Nassar is the Chief of Bariatric Surgery at Fundacion Santa Fe de Bogota, and is a Professor of General Surgery. He is a member of the Association of Obesity and Bariatric Surgery, and the Colombian Surgical Association. After completing his general surgery training at Javeriana University, Dr. Nasser completed his fellowship in advanced gastrointestinal endoscopy surgery at Dundee University in Scotland. He did additional training in gastric band and gastric bypass procedures, and trained in trauma in Pitié-Salpêtrière Hospital[109]. In addition to bariatric procedures, he continues to perform general surgery, including minimally invasive upper gastric surgery, which he also teaches. He has been operating as part of the Santa Fe de Bogota program since 1997[110] and has been the chief of the department for over ten years. He estimates that he has performed over 2,000 surgeries in that time. As part of the bariatric surgery program, he performs lap-band, sleeve gastrectomy and gastric bypass. He is currently involved in an animal study on a new method of gastric bypass to treat obesity more effectively. He anticipates the study will begin by the end of the year (2011.) This study is affiliated with the Cleveland Clinic. At the time of initial interview, Dr. Nasser was

---

[109] This hospital is internationally famous as the site where Princess Diana of Wales died in 1997.

[110] Program was started in 1994.

preparing to deliver a series of lectures at the Latin-American Congress on Obesity and Bariatric Surgery. He is an integral part of the Obesity Center, which has 37 employees on staff. The clinic views bariatric surgery as a tool, not an endpoint in the treatment of obesity. He reports that the average patient embarks on a two-year treatment plan for obesity when coming to the clinic, including evaluations by endocrinologists, internal medical specialists, consultations with physical therapists, nutritionists, and psychiatrists. After initiating a lifestyle change, and medical management, eligible patients are referred for surgical evaluation.

In the operating room, all standardized protocols were followed. Sterility was maintained. Anesthesia coverage was continuous and consistent. Dr. Nasser is relaxed, confident and capable.

Surgical Apgar score: 9
Highly recommended.

Dr. Carlos Saboya, MD
http://www.especialistasenobesidad.com
Calle 108 No. 17A – 68 (one block up from Av 19)
Bogota, Colombia
Tele: 604 – 4841
Email: info@espacialistasenobesidad.com
Emailed, no reply.

Dr. Saboya is a member of the Colombian Association of Obesity and Bariatric Surgery.

The following surgeons were not advertised on television, the internet, or the phonebook. Attempted contact through email addresses provided at the Colombian Society for Obesity and Bariatric Surgery.

Dr. Jaime Hernando Avendano Avilo
Email: jhavendano@gmail.com
Email sent, no reply received.

Dr. William Mauricio Basto Borbon
Email: wbastos@clinicadelcountry.com
Dr. Basto is a general surgeon on staff at Clinica del Country.

General Surgery

Please note that all of the bariatric surgeons listed in the previous section are general surgeons who have chosen to specialize in bariatric surgery. However, currently there is no specialty certification in that area. Many of these bariatric surgeons maintain active general surgery practices in addition to performing bariatric surgery.

Dr. Fernando Arias Amezquita, MD, FACS
Av 9 No. 116 -20 Consultorio 920
Bogota, Colombia
Tele: 215 0405 / 215 3037
Email: faria00@hotmail.com

Emailed to request interview. Dr. Arias is a general surgeon with specialty training in both laparoscopic surgery and cancer treatment, and he is passionate about both. His story is an interesting one and illustrates his love for both his patients and the practice of surgery[111]. In 1998 Dr. Arias graduated from Javeriana after completing his general surgery residency. He then traveled to New York to Sloan Kettering in pursuit of additional laparoscopic training for the treatment of gastric cancers. However, after beginning his fellowship he realized that much of the cancer surgery at Sloan Kettering was still primarily by open incision. At that point he arranged to

---

[111] Part of this story was previously published on-line at Colombia Reports.com on 16 March 2011 in an article entitled, "Bogota hospital offers hope to abdominal cancer patients."

simultaneously receive additional fellowship training at the nearby Presbyterian Hospital in New York. He completed two more years of laparoscopic training and bariatrics at Cleveland Clinic with Dr. Rosenfield. In 2005, he returned and started his practice in Bogota. He specializes in single port laparoscopies for appendectomies, gallbladders and other abdominal surgery. He reports that 90% of his current practice is laparoscopic surgery. One of the cases I observed with Dr. Arias was a case of acute appendicitis requiring appendectomy. I have to say, that in all the cases (and surgeons) I have ever observed, Dr. Arias was truly a joy to watch. He clearly loves his profession, loves surgery and enjoys caring for his patients.

Within forty minutes, the surgery was over, with no visible evidence but for a suture tie from the umbilicus[112]. During all of the cases Dr. Arias followed standardized protocols meticulously, with time-outs to confirm patient, procedure, allergies, antibiotic administration, with pre-operative review pf patient history and available radiographic findings. Aseptic technique was religiously enforced, with excellent and continuous anesthesia coverage.

Dr. Arias, himself is a calm, confident and very talented surgeon. But there is still another side to this caring and compassionate physician. As part of his passion for oncology surgery, Dr. Arias received training and now

---

[112] Belly button.

performs Cytoreductive surgery with intraperitoneal hyperthermic chemotherapy[113].

This procedure, also called the 'Sugarbaker procedure' is used for the treatment of disseminated colo-rectal cancers. This allows doctors to treat patients with disease that has spread throughout the abdomen, which usually carries a very poor prognosis. This process is one of the few ways to aggressively treat a disease that is often otherwise only treated with palliative measures. It is the best chance of survival for these patients.

As Dr. Arias explains, "I had to send a patient out of Colombia for this procedure, and the patient asked, 'why didn't I do the procedure?'. So I decided to." After receiving training in this procedure, Dr. Arias enlisted the aid of Dr. Horotero, an Oncologist, and they began a treatment program in 2009 to treat these patients with this modality. Dr. Arias has performed thirty cases so far[114]107 with encouraging results.

Dr. Arias is a member of multiple surgical societies including the Colombian Surgical Association, International Society of Surgery, Latin American Federation of Surgery, Latin American Association for Transluminal Surgery, European Association for Transluminal Surgery, Society of Laparoscopic Surgeons, and the Society of American Gastrointestinal and

---

[113] Separate article published on HIPEC 16 March 2011, Colombia Reports.com.

[114] As of MArch 2011. There are only 3 sites in Latin America offering this treatment and 14 in the United States.

Endoscopic Surgeons. He is also a fellow in the American College of Surgeons.

He is a Professor of Surgery at the Universidad de Los Andes, and enjoys teaching.

Surgical Apgar scores: 9

Highly Recommended: Dedicated, Skilled, and Caring Surgeon.

Dr. Oswaldo Borraez G
Calle 100 No 14 – 63
Consultorio 502
Bogota, Colombia
Tele: 257 4560
Email: oborraezg@gmail.com

Dr. Borraez is an adjunct professor of surgery at National University. He has been the president of the Colombian Association of Trauma for several years, and former secretary, current vice-president and president-elect for the Colombian Surgical Association. Dr. Borraez attended National University where he is now a professor of surgery.

While Dr. Borraez is technically a trauma surgeon, which is a specialty not covered in this edition, his contributions to both trauma and general surgery specialties should not go overlooked. Dr. Borraez has the distinction of being the inventor of the "Bogota Bag" or "Borraez Bag" which is a plastic film used to cover open abdominal wounds to prevent infection, and compartment syndrome. He first described this treatment while he was a second year surgical resident, training at Hospital San Juan de Dios, in

1984. Prior to this, surgeons had few options for patients with severe abdominal trauma.

Skin closure could be attempted, with resultant swelling of tissues and leakage of fluids from the underlying trauma and surgery, but this often caused compression of blood flow and organ failure[115]. The other option was to leave the abdominal cavity open to allow for the expansion of tissues and fluid leakage. The abdomen was then packed with sterile towels, but this often led to infection and additional problems due to excessive fluid loss as several liters of fluid can be lost through seepage alone. The Bogota Bag, however, is a cheap, readily available plastic film made from sterile fluid container used for urology procedures[116] which both protects the abdominal contents from outside contamination while allowing for expansion, and retaining essential fluids. Dr. Borraez himself describes the utility of this amazingly simple but life-saving idea in an article entitled, "Open Abdomen: the most challenging wound" in the December 2008 issue of Revista Colombiana de Cirugia[117]. The Borraez Bag has been written about in hundreds of articles as well as making its way into standard trauma textbooks such as the one written by Dr. Feliciano, an Atlanta trauma surgeon

---

[115] As the pressure inside the abdomen increases, multiple sequelae develop, as part of the "compartment syndrome". Development of this syndrome leads to multiple organ failure, acute respiratory distress, and often, death.

[116] This is very similar to a bag of intravenous fluids, but larger.

[117] This article is available on-line at: http://www.scielo.unal.edu.co/scielo.php?pid=S2011-75822008000400004&script=sci_arttext

who first learned of the bag as a visiting surgeon to Bogota. Multiple research studies have demonstrated the continued utility of this cheap, but practical technique, which has saved the lives of countless patients who would have otherwise died of compartment syndrome or overwhelming infection. Dr. Borraez, himself, has placed over 1400 Bogota Bags since that fateful day in 1984, including 55 permanent internal placements with no evidence of allergic reactions, increased infection, rejection or other problems[118].

During my visit to Hospital San Blas to see Dr. Borraez, I was able to see several patients with the 'Bogotá bag' in place. Dr. Borraez has also developed a low cost alternative to the pricey wound vacuum systems[119]. His current system uses a natural sponge, a colostomy bag and a suction canister to obtain the same tissue epithelialization and wound healing results but costs less than a dollar per day. These innovations have gained Dr. Borraez an international reputation and speaking engagements worldwide. He could practice at any number of hospitals but instead prefers to stay at Hospital San Blas where he has been for the last twenty seven years, caring for the impoverished, and the homeless of Bogota.

---

[118] Taken from data presented at an international trauma conference in Chile, as presented by Dr. Borraez during an interview.

[119] The 'Wound-Vac' brand by KCI costs several hundred dollars per day to operate.

Dr. Jose Felix Castro B, MD, DipGer
Carrera 16 No 82 – 51
Consultorio 801
Bogota, Colombia
Tele: 616 7822
Email: josefc73@yahoo.com

Dr. Castro speaks English fluently, as well as Italian and his native Spanish. He readily accommodated my request for an interview. Dr. Castro is currently on staff at Clinica del Country as a general and laparoscopic surgeon but has operating privileges at Clinica Ami and Clinica Palermo as well. He attended medical school at Javeriana. After graduation he won a United Nations scholarship to the University of Malta for a one-year program in geriatrics and gerontology. He finished the program magna cum laude before completing a four year general surgery residency with an internship at Louisiana State University. In 2003, while chief resident, he was awarded the National Prize from the Colombian Surgical Association for his work, entitled: "Errors in Health Services: designing safer processes in a University Hospital"[120]. He also has a Master's degree in Health Management from the Universidad de los Andes.

He is a member of the Colombian Surgical Association and the Colombian Association of Bariatric and Metabolic Surgery.

---

[120] A link to the article can be found here: http://www.encolombia.com/medicina/cirugia/Ciru19204-errores.htm (in Spanish).

He has several international patients and maintains a strong email communication with these patients. Dr. Castro reports that he is very customer service oriented and enjoys communicating directly with his patients by whatever media is most convenient for his patients. He is on the American embassy preferred provider list.

Dr. Castro specializes in laparoscopic/ minimally invasive procedures including single port laparoscopy for Nissen fundoplication for the treatment of gastroesophageal reflux disease (GERD), appendectomies, cholecystectomies, and hernia repair. He reports that laparoscopic hernia repair is particularly important because of the reduced amount of post-operative pain for his patients. He also performs sleeve gastrectomies for surgical weight loss.

In the operating room, Dr. Castro is thorough and efficient. All standardized procedures and protocols were followed including a pre-operative "time-out" to confirm patient, procedure, allergies, antibiotic administration and other safety information. He operates with a second surgeon, and sterility was maintained throughout the case. The patient remained hemodynamically stable, with continuous on-site anesthesia monitoring by an anesthesiologist during the entire case. There were no intra-operative or post-operative complications; patients were uneventfully discharged the same day.

Surgical Apgar score: 10
Highly recommended.

Dr. Nathan Bernal Eidelman, MD
Av 9 No 117 – 20
Consultorio 624
Bogota, Colombia
Tele: 214 5473
Email: Nathan.eidelman@ama.com.co
Emailed to request interview, no reply received.
Currently on American embassy list.

Dr. Fabian Emura, MD, PhD
Website: www.emuracenter.org
EmuraCenter LatinoAmerica
Calle 134 No. 7B-83, Piso 1
Edificio El Bosque
Bogota, Colombia
Tel: 627-1493 / 627-1911
E-mail: fabian@emuracenter.org
Dr. Emura is the Founder / CEO and Medical Director of the EmuraCenter and the affiliated Emura Foundation for the promotion of cancer research. Dr. Emura is a general surgeon and gastroenterologist who specializes in the diagnosis and treatment of gastric cancers. Dr. Emura no longer performs general surgery procedures, but focuses his energies on the endoscopic diagnosis and treatment of gastric diseases. In fact, Dr. Emura devised the newest classification system for digestive cancers for which he received international recognition.

Dr. Roosevelt Gomez Fajardo, MD, FACS
Organ Transplant Service
Av 9 No. 116 -20 Consultorio 413
Tele: 215 1938
Email: roosevelt.fajardo@fsfb.edu.co

Dr. Fajardo is the physician I saw during my medical evaluation in Bogota. He was recommended to me by another surgeon, Dr. Hector Pulido, whom I had previously written about.

Dr. Fajardo is a member of the Colombian Surgical Association. He is also a fellow in the American College of Surgeons. Dr. Fajardo specializes in laparoscopic surgery including uniport surgery, and performs a wide range of procedures including transplant, pancreatic and splenic surgery. While Dr. Fajardo is a practicing surgeon, much of his time is divided between surgery and administrative duties at Santa Fe de Bogota. He oversees the residency program with the University of the Andes[121] and is one of the principals behind the affiliation agreement with Johns Hopkins University which was finalized April 7, 2011[122]. He is also the director of the telemedicine program which offers consultations in 14 medicine and surgical specialties for patients living in rural areas[123]. He has authored

---

[121] He is also a Professor of Surgery at the University of the Andes.

[122] Interestingly, Dr. Fajardo describes an 'Institutional branding" agreement which makes no comment on surgical tourism or the outsourcing of American patients. Johns Hopkins University currently has several internationally branded hospitals in Malaysia, Panama and Turkey.

[123] This telemedicine program was featured in El Tiempo, a local newspaper, with print and on-line coverage on April 7, 2011. On-line video

multiple publications in the areas of telemedicine and prevention of post-operative infections.

He is fluent in English, and is exceedingly kind and thoughtful. He is also very thorough. Prior to my arrival in Bogota, he had already reviewed my past medical records, researched my condition and discussed the possible differential diagnoses and treatment options at a multidisciplinary case conference. There was apparently a mix up with the appointment time on the day of my consultation, so the doctor ended up racing up to meet me so I would not have to wait or reschedule. He arrived on time, slightly out of breath to review my case with me. However, despite this relationship, or because of it, it took considerably more effort to observe Dr. Fajardo in the operating room. However, when I was able to reconnect with Dr. Fajardo in the operating room, the case went smoothly.

All pre-operative protocols were followed, including 'time out', with patient confirmation, and verification of time of antibiotic administration. During induction of general anesthesia, the patient briefly became bradycardia (with a heart rate of 35) and hypotensive[124]. However, the anesthesiologist immediately addressed and corrected the situation. The patient was otherwise hemodynamically stable for the remainder of the case. Dr. Carlos Felipe Perdomo assisted during the case. Intra-operatively,

---

reports can be accessed at
http://www.eltiempo.com/Multimedia/especiales/alas/.

[124] This can happen occasionally. More importantly, it was addressed and corrected immediately.

bleeding was well controlled; and the case progressed without incident with no intra-operative complications. In his spare time, Dr. Fajardo enjoys driving his restored World-War Two era Jeep in the hills outside of Bogota.
Surgical Apgar score: 9
Recommended; all protocols followed, surgeon technically proficient.

Dr. Joaquin Adolfo Guerra Nino, MD
Carrera 19 C No. 90- 14
Consultorio 509
Bogota, Colombia
Tele: 610 3793
Email: joardo.gueni@gmail.com

Replied quickly to arrange for interview. Office is across the street from Clinica de la Mujer.

Dr. Guerra speaks some English. He is a member of the International Society of Surgery and the Colombian Surgical Association. He attended National University, graduating in 1979. He completed his general surgery residency in 1982 and has been practicing ever since. He recently scaled back his practice after retiring from Central Police Hospital and the medical tribunal. He was a magistrate for eight years.

He now operates at Clinica de la Mujer, Clinica Palermo and Clinica del Country. He specializes in gastrointestinal surgeries: cholecystectomies, biliary tract surgeries, appendectomies, colonic surgeries, laparoscopic hernia repair, Nissen and other anti-reflux procedures, Heller myotomies/ esophagectomies[125]. In his spare time he enjoys the outdoors on his farm where he grows coffee and keeps livestock, including cows, and spend time with his family.

Dr. Edgar Prieto, MD
Carrera 19 C No. 90 – 30
Consultorio # 507
Bogota, Colombia
Tele:
Email: edgarfprieto@hotmail.com
Responded quickly to schedule an interview.
Speaks Spanish only.
Dr. Prieto is a general surgeon who specializes in liver and biliary surgery. He is a member of the Colombian Surgical Association. He attended Javeriana medical school and completed his residency in general surgery at Javeriana. He is a professor of general surgery at National University. He has been operating for eighteen years, and currently operates at Clinica Palermo, Clinica Marly and Clinica de la Mujer. He performs conventional laparoscopic surgeries including hernia repair, thyroid, colon, biliary and pancreatic surgeries, esophagectomies, cholecystectomies, and Nissen fundoplications. His favorite procedures are biliary surgeries and

---

[125] If you need an esophagectomy, particularly as a treatment for esophageal cancer, please seek a surgeon at a high volume center. This is a high mortality procedure and needs to be performed by a surgeon who performs a minimal of 25 per year. You can contact me through the site for more information.

jejunostomies. When he isn't operating, he enjoys football and tennis. He also likes to travel.

Dr. Prieto initially agreed to observation in the operating room but then asked for hospital clearance with the medical director. Once this was obtained (within less than thirty minutes of his initial request), Dr. Prieto failed to respond to multiple emails to schedule a date to observe surgery.

Dr. Juan Manuel Trancoso de la Ossa, MD and
Dr. Elena Facundo, MD
Email: Tronosso@gmail.com
Tronosso@yahoo.com

Currently looking for new office space.

Both speak excellent English.

Not a member of the Colombian Surgical Association. He (Dr. Trancoso) and several other surgeons report that they decided not to renew membership because they felt the organization provided little service and had poor leadership. Dr. Trancoso finds the lack of cohesiveness among local surgeons disturbing and points to his excellent relationship with Dr. Facundo as an example of how successful business partnerships operate.

Dr. Trancoso de la Ossa is from Mompos, a picturesque Colonial town in Northern Colombia. He currently works at Hospital Santa Clara with his partner, Dr. Elena Facundo . He states that his favorite operation is inguinal hernia repair. Together they are working on several on-going research projects including a project on surgical access in hostile abdomens[126], and another project on determining the optimal timing of colostomy creation in trauma patients. Dr. Trancoso has worked at Santa Clara for four years, and Dr. Facundo, five years respectively. They perform a range of general abdominal surgeries including colostomies and diversions, gastrectomies, hernia repairs, and laparoscopic surgery for appendectomies, cholecystectomies and trauma.

---

[126] Currently, hesitation among surgeons to re-enter a 'hostile' abdomen after infection, adhesions, trauma or other complications leads to increased mortality.

Neurosurgery

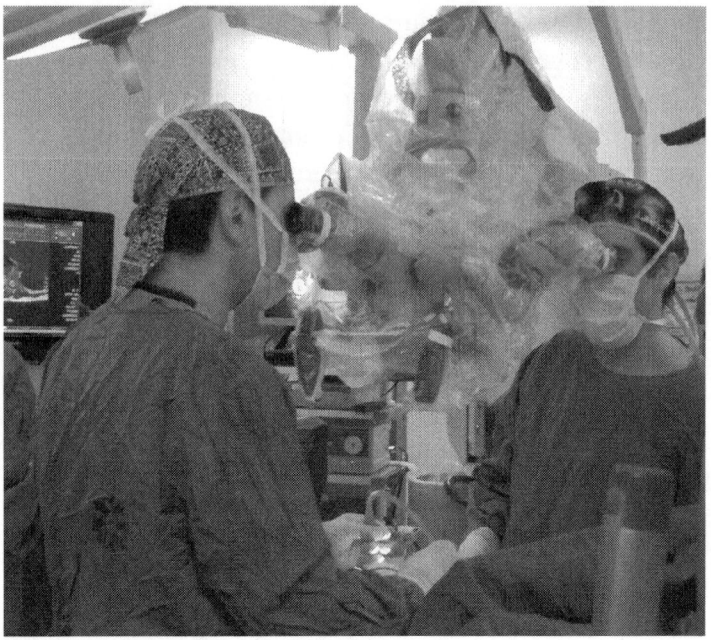

Dr. Hakim operating on a spinal tumor

The practice of neurosurgery has existed for thousands of years, as evidenced by archeological finds demonstrating successful trepanning at several historical sites in the Americas, Europe and the African continent[127]. Modern neurosurgery emerged in the 1950's and 1960's and Bogota

---

[127] A modern day form of trepanning or 'burr holes' still exists. A fascinating history of trepanning from 2003 is available by Dr. Vera Tisler Blos entitled, Cranial Surgery in Ancient Mesoamerica at Mesoweb: <www.mesoweb.com/features/tiesler/Cranial.pdf

neurosurgeons were at the forefront of this. In fact, one of the first successful treatments for hydrocephalus was developedhere in Bogota by a neurosurgery pioneer, Dr. Salomon Hakim[128].

Currently, Bogota remains the headquarters for Colombian neurosurgery. Out of several neurosurgery residency programs, five are located in the capitol. One-third of all Colombian neurosurgeons are practicing within city limits. Within the neurosurgery specialty there are several subspecialties focusing on very specific areas within neurosurgery[129] which are subdivided into: neuroscopic neurosurgery, intracranial neurosurgery, cranial-base neurosurgery, cervical spine specialists and lumbar-thoracic spine specialists. There are also neuronavigational specialists, specializing in the use of neuronavigational technologies and 3-D imaging for localizing and treating cerebral disease.

---

[128] The very first valve for the treatment of hydrocephalus was developed by Dr. Eugene Spitz, an American. However, this shunt often malfunctioned, causing life threatening complications. Dr. Hakim died in May 2011

[129] Subspecialists undergo further education and training (usually fellowships) in their area of subspecialty

Dr. Gerardo Aristizabal Aristizabal, MD
Calle 134 No 7 B – 83
Consultorio 911
Edificio el Bosque
Bogota, Colombia
Tele: 313 283 3051 (cell)
Email: garisti@unbosque.edu.co
gaapen@gmail.com
Emailed to request interview, received no reply.
Dr. Aristizabal is a member of the Colombian Society of Neurosurgery.
He is the Chief of the neurosurgery residency program at Santa Fe de Bogota and Hospital Simon Bolivar.

Dr. Jorge Humberto Aristizabal Maya
Calle 134 No 7 B – 83
Consultorio 911
Edificio el Bosque
Bogota, Colombia
Tele: 301 240 4125 (cell0
Email: jaristabal@cardioinfantil.org
jorari@lycos.com – email returned.
jorgehumbertoa@gmail.com
Emailed to request interview, but received no reply.
Dr. Aristizabal is a member of the Colombian Society of Neurosurgery.

Dr. Juan Antonio Becerra Suarez, MD
Hospital San Jose
Calle 10
Bogota, Colombia
Email: juanabe@hotmail.com
juanabece@gmail.com
Email sent requesting interview, no reply received. Member of the Colombian Society of Neurosurgery. Dr. Becerra is the Chief of the Neurosurgery residency program at Hospital San Jose.

Dr. Jose Luis Buritica Bohorquez, MD
Neurocirugia Clinica San Pedro Claver (Mederi)
Calle 24 No. 29 – 61, Piso 7, Sur
Bogota, Colombia
Tele: 310 375 8827
Email: jlburitica@hotmail.com
Emailed to request interview, no reply received. Both Dr. Buritica and Dr. Cortes are part of the Mederi neurosurgical service, which is the largest in Bogota. Member of the Colombian Society of Neurosurgery.

Dr. Cesar Augosto Buitrago Guzman, MD
Clinica Palermo
Email: cbuitrago@cable.net.co
cbuitrago.epilepsia@gmail.com
Emailed to request interview, no reply received. Member of the Colombian Society of Neurosurgery.

Dr. William Cortes Lozano, MD
Neurocirugia Clinica San Pedro Claver (Mederi)
Calle 24 No. 29 – 61, Piso 7, Sur
Bogota, Colombia
Tele: 300 386 6798
Email: wcortesl@hotmail.com
Emailed to request interview, no reply received.
Member of the Colombian Society of Neurosurgery. There is a record of an official sanction of Dr. Cortes for the death of a patient at Hospital Simon Bolivar; however, on brief review of the case, it appears the patient died from lack of proper supplies, which more accurately reflects on the hospital, not Dr. Cortes. On discovery of the lack of proper equipment to care for this patient, patient should have been transferred to another institution[130]. Given the brevity of information available, and the lack of response from Dr. Cortes to discuss this finding, judgment should be reserved.

Dr. Carlos A. Cure Hakim, MD
Carrera 16 A No. 82 – 46
Consultorio 412
Bogota, Colombia
Tele: 531 1954
Email: cureha@hotmail.com

---

[130] This is what Dr. Cortes was sanctioned for: failure to transfer on April 5, 2005. Record accessed on-line on 6 April 6, 2011 at: http://www.alcaldiabogota.gov.co/sisjur/normas/Norma1.jsp?i=25848 this document illuminates the shortcomings in equipment and staffing at Hospital Simon Bolivar.

Dr. Cure speaks Spanish.

Dr. Cure has been practicing as a neurosurgeon for twenty years. Prior to becoming a surgeon, Dr. Cure studied mechanical engineering and continues to enjoy making model (but functional) robots in his spare time. He went to the Universidad Rosario for medical school and completed his neurosurgical training at Clinica San Rafael. He completed additional coursework at the University of Minnesota. He is a member of the Colombian Association of Neurosurgery.

He reports that approximately 60% of his cases are spinal cases, with the remaining 40% as brain cases. He performs a variety of neurosurgical procedures for aneurysms, brain tumors and related conditions. He also states that while he has endovascular training, he is concerned about the prolonged exposure to radiation that patients receive during these cases, so he prefers conventional surgery in most cases.

Many of his spinal cases are chronic back pain cases, and he reports that his greatest satisfaction is treating and relieving suffering. He believes it is important to talk to patients and establish a good relationship based on trust and mutual respect.

He reports that he has a large amount of American clientele and is on the American Embassy preferred provider list.

Dr. Fernando Hakim Daccach, MD
Av 9 No 116 – 20
Bogota, Colombia
Tele: 629 7503
Email: fhakimd@gmail.com

Email sent requesting interview, responded quickly to schedule appointment.

Dr. Hakim completed his medical and neurosurgical training at Hospital Militar, in the neurosurgery program founded by his father, Dr. Salomon Hakim. He completed his fellowship at Massachusetts General Hospital on the Nicholas service, along with a three month rotation at Brigham Women's and Children's Hospital.

He has been operating since 1992. Dr. Hakim is a member of the Colombian Society of Neurosurgery.

Both he and Dr. Jimenez- Hakim report that the neurosurgery program at Santa Fe de Bogota does not perform neurosurgical treatment for Parkinson's. He reports that he collaborates with orthopedic surgeons for all spinal cases.

While he acknowledges that he is considered the foremost expert in Normal Pressure Hydrocephalus (NPH) diagnosis and treatment in Colombia, he stresses his experience and treatment of a wide range of conditions including vascular abnormalities (arteriovenous malformations, aneurysms), pituitary tumors, spinal and pediatric surgery, traumatic head injuries, malignant and benign brain tumors, neuronavigational and stereotactic surgery. He clearly does not want to be pigeon-holed by his father's work, but is proud of his accomplishments. He has used his father's legacy to further the research and treatment of NPH while maintaining his practice in general neurosurgery.

Dr. Hakim is a high-energy individual who displays a genuine love and interest in his practice and his patients[131]. In the operating room all preoperative protocols and procedures were followed. Dr. Hakim is focused and relaxed, but remains aware of his surroundings. He is an excellent teacher, and explains the painstaking process during the case, while demonstrating excellent attention to detail. Continuous anesthesia & hemodynamic monitoring with no instability.

Surgical Apgar score: 10

Highly recommended.

Dr. Oscar Hernando Feo Lee, MD
Calle 23 No. 66 – 24
Consultorio 916
Bogota, Colombia
Tele: 300 474 1752 (cell)
Email: Feolee@yahoo.com

Email sent, requesting interview. No reply received. Dr. Feo is a member of the American Association of Neurological Surgeons and the Colombian Association of Neurosurgery.

He has several You Tube films showing neuroendoscopic procedures.

---

[131] While Dr. Hakim has been involved in a lawsuit, notably, he along with six others were the plaintiffs (not defendants) in a Texas case involving the sale of securities in 2003.

Dr. Enrique Jimenez Hakim, MD
Av 9 No. 116 – 20
Consultorio 822
Bogota, Colombia
Tele: 629 7094
Email: ejimenezmd@gmail.com

Emailed to request interview; replied quickly to schedule. Speaks fluent English.

He attended medical school at El Rosario. He completed his neurosurgery residency at Hospital Militar in 1986. After completing his residency in Colombia he traveled to the United States where he completed a neurosurgery fellowship at the University of Minnesota with additional training at Massachusetts General Hospital and Boston Children's hospital.

He is currently practicing at Fundacion Santa Fe de Bogota where he is one of four neurosurgeons, and has been Chief of the department of Neurosurgery since 1996. The department of Neurosurgery at Santa Fe de Bogota performs an estimated 500 – 600 cases per year, about equally split between spinal cases and brain tumors, and has partnered with El Bosque for a neurosurgery residency program.

Dr. Jimenez – Hakim has held several offices including President of the Colombian Society of Neurosurgery. He is a professor of neurosurgery at the El Bosque and the University of the Andes.

Dr. Pedro Jose Penagos Gonzalez, MD
Centro Medico Parque 83
Calle 83 No. 19 -36
Consultorio 304
Bogota, Colombia
Tele: 315 331 7215 (his cellular[132])
Email: pjpenagos@hotmail.com

Dr. Penagos responded quickly to an email to schedule a meeting. He speaks English. His office is located two blocks directly behind Clinica del Country on the third floor of a medical office building mainly dominated by dental professionals.

His office waiting room, which is shared with several other physicians, was packed; the presence of patients with CT scans of the head was diagnostic of his patients[133]. I had to endure a lengthy wait, but it was readily apparent that Dr. Penagos is a chronically busy surgeon – with a wilted, forgotten barely disturbed lunch on his test as testament to his practice. He reports long days are the norm, starting at five am until ten pm. His annual surgical volume of 600 cases per year attests to this, as well as a glance at the receptionist's appointment book.

---

[132] Most doctors in Colombia readily provide cellular numbers, which I have omitted in most cases. However, Dr. Penagos shares a receptionist with eight other doctors so his cellular number is provided for your convenience.

[133] Making it easy to differentiate his patients from patients of the other physicians which were a psychiatrist, several opthalmogists and ondontologists

Dr. Penagos is the Chief of the National Institute of Cancer and specializes in treatment of brain tumors including both primary brain cancers and metastases.

He reports that he resected over 300 brain and spinal tumors last year. He also performs surgery for a wide range of spinal conditions including trauma, degenerative diseases, infections and vascular malformations.

He is currently operating at Colsanitas Reina Sofia, Clinica del Country and Clinica Palermo.

Dr. German Pena Quinones
Ave 9, No 116 – 20
Consultorio 417
Bogota, Colombia
Tele: 215 0341
Email: germanpenamd@hotmail.com

Emailed to request interview.

Dr. Pena works in the neurosurgery department at Santa Fe de Bogota. He is a professor of neurosurgery at the Universidad el Bosque. He has held several positions in the neurosurgery community including the former president, and vice president of the Colombian Association of Neurosurgery.

He is the former secretary general, and vice president of the National Academy of Medicine for Colombia. He also served as president of the XXVI Latin American Congress of Neurosurgery and served on the executive committee. He is an active international member of the American

Association of Neurological Surgeons[134], Congress of Neurological Surgery, and serves on the executive committee of the World Federation of Neurological Societies. He graduated from a Colombian medical school in 1964 and completed his neurosurgery training in 1973. He also received a certificate for the Mayo Graduate School of Medicine.

Dr. Juan Fernando Ramon Cueller, MD
www.neuromin.com
Av 9 No. 116 – 20
Consultorio 822
Bogota, Colombia
Tele: 629 7094

Website with English language version, and toll-free number for North American patients. Dr. Ramon speaks some English.

Dr. Ramon specializes in minimally invasive neurosurgery, and intracranial procedures. He is one of a handful of surgeons in Colombia to perform neuroendoscopy.

Dr. Ramon attended medical school at National University in Bogota, and completed his residency at El Bosque. He completed his neurosurgery fellowship at the University of Miami, and additional training at Brigham Women's and Children's hospital in Boston.

---

[134] Unable to verify with the American Association of Neurological Surgeons.

He is a member of the Colombian Society of Neurosurgery[135], the International Federation of Neuroendoscopy and AOSpine.

Dr. Ramon currently operates at Fundacion Santa Fe de Bogota, Hospital Centro de Policia and Clinica el Bosque. At the time of our initial interview, Dr. Ramon was preparing to give a presentation at a conference in Mexico. He had also arranged for a patient consultation, after being contacted by a patient in Mexico for further evaluation to prevent the patient from incurring additional costs related to travel.

Dr. Mauricio Toscano Heredia
Carrera 13 No 49 -40
Consultorio 320, Clinica Marly
Bogota, Colombia
Email: mtoscanohe@yahoo.com
Email sent requesting interview, no reply.

Dr. Toscano is a member of the Colombian Association of Neurosurgery.

---

[135] Unable to verify current membership.

Orthopedics

Dr. Sergio Abello, MD
http//:www.feetcenter.com.co
Feet Center
Carrera 19A No 90 – 13
Bogota, Colombia
Tele: 691 8544
Email: abello.sergio@gmail.com

Speaks English fluently. Dr. Sergio Abello is a very pleasant and friendly orthopedic surgeon specializing in care of the foot and ankle.

Dr. Abello attended the University of British Colombia before returning to Colombia to attend medical school. While in training, he received a research award from Adventis for his work on the reconstruction of defects in porcine models. He graduated from his specialty training (orthopedics) with honors from El Bosque in 2002. He did additional specialty training at the Weil Foot and Ankle Institute in Chicago, Illinois.

As part of his services, he offers computerized, completely customized orthotic inserts. He also used the software to diagnose and measure post-procedure results in many of his patients. I tested this software during a visit to his office. The software works by measuring the feet, the stride, pressure points and several other parameters. It then generates a 3-D reconstruction of the foot that is used to create personalized orthopedic inserts to treat and prevent a variety of foot conditions.

Dr. Abello takes American insurance plans and has an international patient program. Most patients stay on average 10 – 15 days, depending on procedure. His office coordinates all arrangements as needed.

In his spare time Dr. Abello enjoys mountain biking, riding motorcycles off-roads and swimming.

The first three cases I observed with Dr. Abello at Clinica Shaio went exceptionally well, except for hypotension which was roundly ignored despite attempting to direct attention to it[136]. The fourth case, which to be fair, was a very difficult case (a young man with a history of a previous crush injury to his left foot, who was here for a last salvage attempt of the limb) initially began well. The nurse covering for anesthesia maintained hemodynamic stability during the entire case, sterility was maintained, pre-operative films reviewed and all other protocols followed. But at the time of primary incision closure, the patient began bleeding a steady stream[137]. Instead of re-exploring and controlling the bleeding from (what I suspect was) a vascular laceration with cautery, clips or ligation, Dr. Abello did not definitively address the continued bleeding and increased his efforts to close the incision. He used a small amount of surgi-cel, a chemical hemostatic agent, but he did not place a drain[138] or seek

---

[136] While there is a possibility that the readings were in error during these cases, no attempts were made to check the blood pressure cuffs, recalibrate machinery or verify the actual blood pressure of these three separate patients

[137] Orthopedic cases can be quite bloody but this was in excess of what was to be expected.

[138] To evacuate the growing hematoma and detect continued bleeding.

treat the source of problem. Following wound closure, the wound continued to leak a steady stream of bright blood, and the foot showed signs of a growing hematoma, which was confirmed by a post-operative x-ray. This placed the patient at risk for compartment syndrome, and potential loss of limb, as well as blood loss complications. While the patient was reported to make unremarkable recovery, the case remains concerning.

Surgical Apgar scores: 7 for initial cases. Final case: 4
Orthotics services recommended.

Dr. Francisco Jose Cabal, MD
http://orthodoc.aaos.org/DRCABAL/
Unidad Medica Nueva - Clinica del Country
Calle 16A No 82 – 46
Consultorio 202
Bogota, Colombia
Tele: 610 – 6265
Email: fcabal@hotmail.com

Emailed to request interview; received timely reply to schedule appointment. Dr. Cabal speaks English and Italian as well as his native Spanish.

Website maintained by American Association of Orthopedic Surgeons (AAOS) in English. Dr. Cabal is a fellow in this organization, international affiliate.

Dr. Cabal is the Chairman of the Orthopedics department at Clinica del Country and is the International Advisor for this institution as well as the Board of Directors. Dr. Cabal is on the preferred provider list for the American and

British Embassies[139] and has received several commendations for his service to the personnel of the embassy as well as President George W. Bush during his visit to Colombia in 2007. He is also the European Affairs Advisor, so he was responsible for establishing an international patient program at Clinica del Country.

He has been performing orthopedic surgery, primarily hip and knee surgery, since 1995. He performs approximately 200 surgeries per year and reports that he takes a fairly conservative approach initially, before planning surgery. "It is more important to do surgery at the right time [when the patient will benefit] than to just do surgery."

He currently accepts Blue Cross, Blue Shield, Cigna and several other American insurances. He also works with Medicare, and is developing an agreement with Medicare and JCI institutions[140].

During the case, Dr. Cabal was assisted by Dr. Jaime Rojas. In the operating room at Clinica del Country, all standardized protocols such as a pre-operative time out, proper patient positioning, and on-time antibiotic administration were performed. There was continuous anesthesia monitoring, and vital signs remained within an acceptable range.

Bleeding was well-controlled, and the case proceeded

---

[139] Dr. Cabal's wife, Dr. Claudia Zoppi is a general practitioner (internist) at the British Embassy. Dr. Francisco Cabal serves as the Post-Medical Advisor of the US Embassy.

[140] The regulations surrounding Medicare add a level of complexity to the paperwork, but he readily accepts Medicare patients

without complications[141].
Surgical Apgar score: 7
Recommended.

Dr. German Carillo Arango, MD
AK 9 No 116 – 20
Consultorio 815
Bogota, Colombia
Tele: 620 3079
Email: germancarilloarango@gmail.com
Emailed to request interview; no reply received.
Dr. Carillo completed both his medical training and orthopedic residency at Javeriana University.

Dr. Ramon Herrera De Bedout, MD
Av 9 No 116 – 20
Consultorio # 716
Bogota, Colombia
Tele: 620 3210
Email: ramon.debedout@ama.com.co
Emailed to request interview; no reply received.
Dr. Herrera completed medical school, orthopedic residency and subspecialty training in hand and microsurgery at Javeriana University. Currently on American embassy list.

---

[141] Orthopedic cases have the potential for significant bleeding as bone is well supplied with blood, and bone tissue is surrounded by blood vessels, nerves and other tissues.

Dr. Maria Angela Gomez Martinez
Calle 80 No 10 – 43
Consultorio 506
Bogota, Colombia
Tele: 218 6539
Email: lagoda3@hotmail.com
Speaks fluent English.

Dr. Gomez is a dually trained surgeon and works as both a hand surgeon and a plastic surgeon. She attended Javeriana for medical school, followed by plastic surgery/orthopedic residency at El Rosario[142]. She completed a fellowship in hand surgery in France. Dr. Gomez has twenty years experience in her specialty practices and enjoys the variety that her dual practice provides. As a hand surgeon, she operates as an orthopedic surgeon at Clinica San Rafael several days a week, performing traumatic injury repair, digital re-implantation and pursuing her research interests in the endemic occupational injuries sustained by women with small hands.

She reports that this chronic problem is particularly widespread among the floral industry here in Colombia, which is predominantly female occupation requiring heavy lifting[143]. Currently she is collecting information to

---

[142] This speciality pairing is not uncommon, and is actually a subspecialty of orthopedics but it is less common to see surgeons maintaining separate practices devoted to both plastics and orthopedics.

[143] Colombian women, on average, are several inches smaller than their North American counterparts, with corresponding small extremities, which predisposes these women to several types of hand injuries.

develop a scale to classify hand size, and risk of occupational injury in coordination with SaludCoop and the public health department.

In her plastic surgery practice at Clinica de Marly, she performs a wide range of procedures including reconstructive procedures after trauma and cancer surgeries, breast augmentation/ reduction, abdominoplasties, and other corporal procedures, face and eye-lifts. She does not perform rhinoplasty or lipectomy.

Instituto de Orthopedia y Cirugia Plastica
http://www.ortopediayplastica.com
Av 19 No 114 – 87
Bogota, Colombia
Tele: 619 0311
Email: pacientes@ortopediayplastica.com

Sent emails via website; received reply declining interview. I attempted to contact several different surgeons from this group for a possible interview but received no further replies.

Website with English version.

This is a large multiple specialty surgical group. There are seven orthopedic surgeons and five plastic surgeons[144].

Dr. Oswaldo Lazula Vargas is the director of the practice.

Dr. Cesar Alvarado Garcia, MD is a member of the Colombian Society of Orthopedic and Trauma Surgery, and former President of the Hospital Militar. He performs a wide range of orthopedic procedures.

---

[144] Plastic surgeons are listed separately in the plastic surgery chapter.

Dr. Nelson Reyes Bocanegra, MD performs a wide range of orthopedic procedures.
Dr. Juan Alberto Pineros Camacho, MD is a member of the Colombian Society of Orthopedic and Trauma Surgery.
Dr. Oswaldo Lazula Vargas, MD, (mentioned above) is member of multiple organizations including; the Colombian Society of Orthopedic and Trauma Surgery.
Dr. Carlos Alejandro Perez Rubio, MD
Dr. Diego Alfredo Rozo Garcia, MD
Dr. Catherine Reyes Rodriguez, MD
Dr. Carlos Arturo Roso Moncada is the anesthesiologist for the practice who also specializes in pain management.

Dr. Angela Rocio Hernandez Arenas, MD
Email: arhernandez@cardioinfantil.org
Email promptly bounced. Dr. Hernandez is a member of the Colombian society of Orthopedic and Trauma surgery, but there was no additional contact information. Internet search failed to reveal any additional information.

Dr. Mauricio Largacha Ponce de Leon, MD
www.mauriciolargacha.com
Carrera 16 A No 82 – 46
Consultorio 402
Bogota, Colombia
Tele: 531 4090
Email: Mauriciolargacha@hotmail.com
Emailed to request interview; replied promptly to schedule. Speaks fluent English.

Dr. Largacha attended Javeriana University medical school and completed his orthopedic residency at Santa Fe de Bogota. He then completed a fellowship in elbow and shoulder arthroscopy at the Mayo Clinic in Rochester for seven months with an additional five months in Seattle, Washington.

Dr. Largacha operates at Clinica del Country, Reina Sofia, and Unidad Clinica Cecimin. He is a member of the Colombian Society of Orthopedic and Trauma Surgery, and specializes in shoulder and elbow surgery. Dr. Largacha is the former chairman of hand and elbow surgery for the VI Latin American forum (2009). He has written several chapters of orthopedic textbooks, particularly on elbow reconstruction, including American medical textbooks. He teaches arthroscopy techniques throughout Latin America, and reports that advances in shoulder and elbow arthroscopy have led to drastically better surgical outcomes in the last ten years.

He performs approximately 350 procedures a year, including: arthroscopy, joint replacement, rotator cuff repair and other procedures involving the elbow and shoulder. He believes strongly in subspecialization within orthopedic surgery due to the increased complexity of surgery of the shoulder and elbow.

In the operating room all pre-operative procedures and protocols were followed, including application of antiembolic devices, proper patient positioning/ sterile draping, time put procedures and antibiotic administration. Sterility was maintained throughout the case. Anesthesia was excellent with a combination of

general anesthesia and a regional block for post-operative pain control. There was continuous anesthesia monitoring during the case with no alterations in hemodynamic status. Dr. Largacha was relaxed and confident during the case and demonstrated considerable expertise. The case progressed quickly with no complications.
Surgical Apgar score: 9
Highly recommended: experienced subspecialist.

Dr. Victor Hugo Lizcano Ortit
Calle 91 No. 19C – 51
Consultorio 308
Bogota, Colombia
Email: vhlizcano@hotmail.com
Departmento de Ortopedia y Traumatologia
Hospital Clinica San Rafael
Carrera 8A No 17 – 45 Sur
Bogota, Colombia

Dr. Lizcano is the Chief of Orthopedic Surgery at the Clinica San Rafael which is a large subspecialty orthopedic clinic with 11 orthopedic surgeons, 10 of which are subspecialists.

The department of orthopedics maintains a clinic on the ground floor of the hospital in addition to private offices for several of the surgeons. The Orthopedic Surgery division at San Rafael has been nationally and internationally recognized throughout Latin America for surgical excellence. The department boasts of four former presidents of the Colombian Society of Orthopedic and Trauma Surgery, two presidents of the national scientific society and the current president of the Latin American Society of Orthopedics & Trauma Surgeons.

Dr. Lizcano reports that while Clinica San Rafael currently has no medical tourism program, interested patients should contact his department directly for assistance.

Dr. Lizcano is originally from Bucaramanga in the Santander region of Colombia but came to Bogota to study medicine.

He attended Javeriana, and completed his orthopedic residency at the University Militar (Clinica San Rafael). He specializes in sports medicine and knee surgery including arthroscopy and total joint replacement. He has been operating for over fifteen years and operates at both Clinica San Rafael and SaludCoop.

During the case, the patient received only regional anesthesia and was awake and conversant during the procedure. The patient appeared comfortable and denied pain during the procedure; however, this scenario limits the applicability of the surgical Apgar scoring system. The patient was hemodynamically stable during the case. All pre-operative procedures and protocols were followed; sterility was maintained during the case. There was no significant intra-operative bleeding or other complications. *Surgical Apgar* score not applicable for this case.
Recommended.

Dr. Klaus Mieth Alviar, MD
Calle 119A No 7 – 91 (bone bank address)
Bogota, Colombia
Tele: 658 3200
Carrera 9 No 116 – 20 (patient consultation office)
Consultorio # 717
Bogota, Colombia
Tele: 215 2737
Email: Klaus@cydbank.org
Emailed to request interview; responded in a timely manner.

Dr. Mieth is fluent in English, German and Spanish.

Dr. Mieth is an orthopedic surgeon specializing in hip reconstruction and knee arthroscopy / surgery. He attended Javeriana University medical school and completed orthopedic residency and subspecialty training in hip and knee surgery at Javeriana in 1995. He received a Master's in Clinical Epidemiology from Javeriana in 2007.

Dr. Mieth is also the Director of the largest Bone and tissue[145](muscle, tendons) bank in Colombia. This non-profit organization provides bone and tissue for Colombians requiring reconstructive procedures. These tissues are provided free of cost to indigent patients. On occasion, for humanitarian reasons, bone and tissue are sent to neighboring countries such as Venezuela or Ecuador. Dr. Mieth is very proud of the high quality of the donations and the processing at this clinic. In fact, he

---

[145] No skin or heart valves processed at this tissue bank.

wrote much of the textbook for national guidelines for establishing protocols for clinical practice here in Colombia. He is involved with Colsciencias, which is a national research institute developed to evaluate and analyze the quality of research being conducted in Colombia. Despite all of this, Dr. Mieth reports that orthopedic surgery remains his primary focus and states he performs an average of 3 to 5 cases per week as a staff surgeon at Santa Fe de Bogota.

While Dr. Mieth has training in hip surgery, he primarily performs knee procedures such as joint replacement and arthroscopy.

Dr. Catalina Morales, MD
http://www.catalinamoralesplasticos.com
Carrera 19 A No. 90 – 13
Consultorio 506
Bogota, Colombia
PBX: 616 0961
Email: Catalina_mr@hotmail.com

Dr. Catalina Morales is a dually trained plastics and hand surgeon. She has been studying English and speaks some English in preparation for a trip to England to study new treatments in hand surgery.

Dr. Morales completed medical school and a four year residency in plastic, aesthetic, reconstructive, hand and maxillofacial surgery at National University. During her residency, she received recognition from the Colombian Society of Plastic and Reconstructive Surgery as the top resident in Colombia. She maintains current membership with that organization.

She currently operates at La Clinica Carlos Lleras Restrepo, Clinica de Marly and in Chia, at Hospital Teleton, as she maintains a multi-specialty clinic for her patients in Chia. She states that she always enjoyed the surgical specialties during her medical training because of the feeling of being able to resolve a specific problem for her patients. She enjoyed her surgery professors who encouraged her to subspecialize in plastic and reconstructive surgery. She enjoys the variety in her day to day practice. She states she gets the greatest professional satisfaction from her reconstructive work, particularly cleft-palate repair in children, or post-cancer reconstruction but likes being able to improve the lives of all her patients through increased self-esteem and happiness in their appearances. She pursued additional training in hand surgery because she enjoys the complexity of the cases.

In her spare time she likes to read books of any genre but particularly novels and classic literature.

During my visits to the operating room with Dr. Morales, she had several hand surgeries scheduled. All of these cases were repair after traumatic amputations. As Dr. Morales explained, occupational injuries causing severe trauma and digit loss are fairly common industrial accidents among the blue collar workers here. In fact, one of the patients I spoke with, a very nice, very young man who had lost several fingers in this type of accident, told me that his best friend had a similar accident four months

previously. It was heartbreaking speaking to this young man during the case, but it highlighted the importance of Dr. Morales' (and other hand surgeons) work. All of the hand surgery cases were done under a combination of slow acting and immediate acting local anesthetic for longer post-operative pain control. The patients were awake and conversant during the case[146] and reported good pain relief. Pre-operative films and cases were reviewed prior to surgery, and all surgical protocols were followed. Sterility was maintained during the cases. Dr. Morales was pleasant, and open with the patients during the cases, and painstakingly meticulous in her attempts to salvage tissue, and preserve functionality.
Recommended. A talented young doctor.

Dr. Constanza Lucia Moreno Serrano, MD
Carrera 9 No 116 – 20
Consultorio 519
Bogota, Colombia
Tele: 214 8370
Email: clmorenos@yahoo.com
Email sent to request interview; replied in a timely fashion. Dr. Moreno is an orthopedic surgeon specializing in hand and microsurgery. After graduating from Javeriana University and completing her orthopedic residency in 2001, Dr. Moreno completed her fellowship in hand, microsurgery and microvascular surgery at the renown Kleinert Hand Center in Louisville, Kentucky. She

---

[146] Making the Apgar score inapplicable.

finished her training in 2005 and has been operating at Santa Fe de Bogota since then.

She specializes in the treatment of traumatic injuries including digital and limb reconstruction, correction of congenital deformities and other forms of surgical reconstruction. She is currently developing a protocol for the creation of a Hand Transplant program at Santa Fe de Bogota[147]. She aims to be able to treat the Colombian victims of landmine injuries with this center.

Dr. Javier Perez Torres, MD
http://www.slaot.org
Calle 134 No 7B – 83
Oficina 201
Bogota, Colombia
Tele: 625 7445
Email: japetohip@yahoo.com
comunicaciones@slaot.org

Dr. Javier Perez is the current Presidential delegate of the Latin America Society of Orthopedic and Trauma Surgeons (SLAOT). He operates at Clinica San Rafael with Dr. Victor Lizcano.

---

[147] At the time of our initial interview, 23 hand transplants had been performed worldwide.

Dr. Martha Lucia Pinzon, MD
Departmento Ortopedia y Traumatologia
Hospital Clinica San Rafael
Carrera 8A No 17 – 45 Sur
Bogota, Colombia

Dr. Pinzon specializes in foot and ankle surgery. She is a Bogota native and completed her specialty training at Clinica San Rafael. She has been operating for eight years and is pursuing further training in ankle replacement surgery.

In the operating room, Dr. Pinzon is competent and focused. The patient was awake and conversant during the case after receiving a regional block. The patient appeared comfortable during the case, and denied pain. All procedures and protocols were followed with serial radiographs taken and examined during the procedure to ensure proper pin placement. Sterility was maintained, and there was no significant bleeding or hemodynamic changes during the case.

Recommended. Apgar score not applicable.

Dr. George Felipe Ramirez, MD
Email: presidente@slaot.org

No reply received to email request for interview. Dr. Ramirez is currently the President of the Latin American Society of Orthopedic and Trauma Surgeons.

Dr. Gilberto Sanguino Torrado, MD
Email: gsanguin@claustro.urosario.edu.cc

Emailed to request interview. Email bounced. Unable to find additional contact information.

Dr. Jaime Enrique Segura Duran, MD
Email: jesugu@gmail.com
Encountered Dr. Segura during a chance meeting in the hallways of Clinica del Country. At that time we exchanged contact information to arrange for a more formal meeting. I emailed Dr. Segura for a more formal interview request, but never received a reply.
Dr. Segura is a member of the Colombian Society of Orthopedic and Trauma Surgery.

Plastic Surgery

It is important to note that while North American beauty ideals are constantly evolving, they can differ significantly from Latin American standards of beauty, which can appear exaggerated to North Americans. In general this often means bigger breast implants, larger lip plumping, and a larger variety of procedures overall.

Be sure to bring photographs and to clearly communicate your thoughts to your surgeon using a translator if necessary. Be realistic in your expectations for outcomes and be sure to bring a list of questions. Ask to see before and after photographs of incisions and specific procedures. All surgical procedures create scars, and the size and placement of surgical incisions depends on the procedure performed and the technique used. In general procedures such as breast reduction and abdominoplasty create larger scars than liposuction or face-lifts. These scars are sometimes, but not always, hidden in the scalp or natural skin folds. However, there can be significant residual scars from some of these procedures. This should be a point of discussion with you and your surgeon prior to undertaking any surgical procedures to prevent false expectations or unwanted outcomes.

Plastic surgery is often used after bariatric surgery for excess skin removal, and some surgeons advertise these procedures for weight loss. However, while corporal procedures may drastically change a person's appearance, in general, none of these procedures produces actual weight loss, akin to bariatric procedures.

In South America, Brazilian trained surgeons are considered superior to all others, and South Americans utilize plastic surgery more commonly than most people from the United States.

Lists of procedures below are not all-inclusive and may change. Please contact the clinics below for more information regarding pricing and procedures.

Several of the local plastic surgeons that I spoke with included sightseeing trips on the first two days on Bogota, along with face to face consultation. These particular doctors required patients to have at least two days to become acclimatized to the altitude prior to undergoing any surgical procedures.

Please limit your plastic surgery plans to one or two procedures per surgical trip. Additional operating room time incurs additional surgical risk. A very safe two hour procedure becomes incrementally more dangerous as it morphs into a ten hour multi-procedure event.

Another note of caution regarding injectables such as Botox: while these are widely available outside of physicians' offices, in places such as hair and nail salons, please use good judgment and commonsense. These treatments are not entirely benign in nature[148], and since the purpose of injectables is cosmetic, be sure to see a licensed plastic surgeon or dermatologist for optimal results.

---

[148] Botox is botulism toxin, and in worse-case scenarios, improperly used Botox has been linked to respiratory failure. More commonly, improperly injected Botox gives the patient a frozen or drooped appearance similar to a person after a hemiplegic stroke.

Aesthetic Medical Spa
Dr. Umar Abello, MD
www.cirugiaestheticaylaser.com
Cr. 10 No. 96 – 25
Consultorio 403
Tele: 616 0557
Alt. tele: 616 0574

Emailed to request interview; no reply received. On-line website with English version details aesthetic and plastic surgery procedures including facial lifts, rhinoplasty, eye lifts, other facial plastic surgery as well as multiple body procedures; breast procedures, genital surgeries (vaginoplasty, labioplasty), abdominal procedures (tummy tuck). They also perform bariatric procedures including gastric bypass and intra-gastric balloon. They perform hair transplants, pectoral implants and gluteal augmentation for men.

This clinic also specializes in nonsurgical treatments such as laser treatments for facial rejuvenation, scar removal and hair removal. They also perform nonsurgical cellulite treatments such as ultrasonic liposuction. The Aesthetic Medical Spa also coordinates medical travel packages for international patients.

The American Institute de Cirugia Plastica
Dr. Rito Marino, MD
www.americanestetica.com
Calle 83 No 19 – 36 Consultorio 702-703
Bogota, Colombia
(57 1) 616 5506
Email: info@americanestetica.com

Emailed to request interview. Dr. Marino replied to first email in a timely fashion to arrange for an interview. I am disappointed to report that after scheduling an appointment by phone, then confirming the appointment the day before, I waited several hours one afternoon waiting to speak with Dr. Marino. First, the receptionist informed me after my arrival that my appointment had to be moved to another time[149]. Then after I returned at the designated time, an hour later, she refused to acknowledge me. After waiting another hour with no further acknowledgement, I left. Dr. Marino failed to respond to subsequent attempts to contact him.

Website in Spanish only. Dr. Marino speaks English. Dr. Marino is a member of the Colombian Society of Plastic Surgery. He performs the full range of surgical procedures from facial procedures such as face lifts, eye-lifts, rhinoplasty, chin / cheek implants, injectables, etc. along with a full complement of body procedures: breast

---

[149] It appeared to be in an arbitrary fashion; no excuses or explanations made. As a healthcare provider, I know that emergencies and unavoidable delays can occur, but there was no indication of this. Surgeons are busy, but your time is important, particularly if you have traveled a great distance to see the doctor.

procedures, liposuction, abdominal sculpting, genital surgeries for men and women, pectoral and gluteal implants, hair restoration, thigh and calf implants, and several other procedures.

Dr. Marino also offers medical tourism packages including surgery, recovery, hotel and sightseeing.

Dr. Ernesto Andrade, MD
http://www.ernestoandrade.com/
Carrera 19 No 90 – 59
Bogota, Colombia
Tele: 530 5925
Email: info@ernestoandrade.com

Emailed to request interview. Granted a limited interview with Dr. Eliana Garces, a physician awaiting placement in a plastic surgery residency. However, despite agreeing to allow me to observe surgery for this project, neither Dr. Garces nor Dr. Andrade ever returned subsequent phone calls.

Dr. Celso Bohorquez Escobar, MD
Diagonal 115 A No 70 C – 75
Clinica Shaio
Bogota, Colombia
Tele: 296 – 5035
Email: estetiplas@hotmail.com
esteticaplastica@gmail.com

Email sent requesting interview.

Met Dr. Bohorquez in person at the hospital in Chia. Dr. Bohorquez was part of the plastic surgery team operating on several small children that day for correction of cleft palate, as part of Operacion Sonrisa (Operation Smile). Dr. Bohorquez is heavily advertised on the internet as part of the listings for several medical tourism companies, including Turismedic, where he is listed as the Director of Plastic Surgery[150]. He was also interviewed for a feature story in the Houston Chronicle several years ago about "budget plastic surgery[151].

Dr. Celso Bohorquez is a member of the Colombian Society of Plastic Surgery and a member of the Board of Directors.

Dr. Bohorquez attended medical school and completed his general surgery residency at Juan C. Corpus. He completed his plastic surgery residency in Brazil at Hospitales los Clinicas in San Paolo with Dr. Marcos Castro. He also completed additional training in facial endoscopy and now teaches these techniques to other physicians in South America. He is currently a professor of plastic surgery at Juan C. Corpus, and has been practicing at Clinica Shaio for twenty-nine years, since completing his training.

Dr. Bohorquez performs both reconstructive plastic surgery and aesthetic procedures. One of his specialties is reconstructive plastic surgery for congenital

---

[150] The title seems excessive, as he is also the only plastic surgeon listed for Turismedic The title seems excessive, as he is also the only plastic surgeon listed for Turismedic.

[151] Otis, J. (2 Dec 2007) 'Sun, Surf and Scalpels: Colombia's budget plastic surgery." Available on-line at:
http://www.chron.com/disp/story.mpl/world/5343450.htm

malformations, particularly of the face. As part of this, he has been volunteering with Operacion Sonrisa for over fifteen years.

He also enjoys performing aesthetic corporal procedures. He does enforce a three day waiting period for people unused to the elevated altitude of Bogota, and offers medical tourism services for his out-of-town patients. In person Dr. Bohorquez is genial, relaxed with a great sense of humor. In his spare time he enjoys cooking.

When operating, Dr. Bohorquez performs all his procedures under general anesthesia[152]. He does not perform any procedures in the office, because he feels that clinic procedures are inherently less safe and less sterile than the operating room.

In the operating room, all pre-operative procedures and protocols were followed. However, despite one case being quite lengthy, no compression devices or anti-embolic stockings were used. Anesthesia monitoring was fairly consistent; the anesthesiologist did leave during the cases but for very short periods of time and remained just outside the door. However, the telemetry and hemodynamic monitor was not visible to the surgeon during the case, and was turned facing in the opposite direction. There were no prolonged periods of hypotension, but there were brief periods (5 to 10 minutes) when blood pressure dipped into the 70's systolic.

---

[152] In contrast to some physicians who perform some or all procedures under conscious sedation or local anesthesia.

Dr. Bohorquez was relaxed and confident. He demonstrated superior skill, particularly during the facial endoscopy procedure. (Facial endoscopy was performed as part of a face-lift procedure and involves making small incisions above the hairline, in the scalp, for access to superficial and deep muscles of the face, for lifting, and anchoring of facial tissues for a more youthful appearance.) There were no intra-operative complications, and both patients demonstrated excellent cosmetic results at the conclusion of the cases.

Surgical Apgar score: 7

Recommended, excellent surgeon, but concerns related to hemodynamic monitoring during cases.

Centro de Cirugia Estetica
Dr. Julio Gil Antorveza
www.plastiestetica.com

2 clinics:
Clinica Navarra:
Autopisa Norte No. 106– 30 Cons: 601-602
PBX: 523 9262
Fax: 523 9325
tele 522 3546
Centro Medico Horizonte:
Av. Calle 127 No. 20 – 78 Piso 1
PBX: 627 – 0111
alt. 626-9522
Emailed to request interview; no reply.

Dr. Gil is a member of the Colombian society of Plastic Surgeons. On-line website details the procedures offered in his ambulatory clinic including face lifts, eye-lifts, rhinoplasty, liposuction, breast procedures, abdominal / gluteal procedures (i.e. Tummy tuck, butt-lift, etc.) as well as procedures especially marketed to men such as breast tissue reduction, and gluteal augmentation. They also offer Botox and other injectables.
Website in Spanish only.

Centro International de Cirugia Plastica
Dr. Javier Carlos Carranza, MD
www.bellezacorporal.com
Ave. Pepe Sierra Calle 116 No 16 – 45
Bogota, Colombia
571 215 7848
Email: belleza.corporal@hotmail.com
Emailed to request interview; no reply.
Dr. Carranza is a member of the Colombian Society of Plastic Surgeons.
Website with English version. Offers a variety of facial and body procedures including face, eye lifts, check and chin implants, facial liposuction for double chins and large cheeks, rhinoplasty, ear pinning. Body procedures include breast procedures, abdominal liposuction, body sculpting, and gluteal implants.

Ciencia y Estetica Cirugia Plastica
Dr. Luis Pavajeau Munoz
http://www.cirugiaesteticaencolombia.com/English
http://www.cienceyesthetica.com
Carrera 17 No. 116 - 55
Bogota, Colombia
Tele: 620 6830
Email: pavajeauluis@yahoo.com
Emailed to request interview.
Website in English.

Dr. Pavajeau bills himself on the internet as "The Best Plastic Surgeon in Bogota, Colombia" and "The Best Plastic Surgeon in the World." His website is heavily geared towards medical tourism with slogans such as "Everything will come easier if you look good" and descriptions and price listings for medical packages. He also has several YouTube videos about his clinic with patient testimonials[153]. He speaks English and French, in addition to Spanish.

Given these claims, I was prepared to dislike or at least disregard Dr. Pavajeau, but instead found him to be very informative and patient safety oriented. During interviews with physicians, I always ask for information to pass along to my readers. Dr. Pavajeau actually took his time to consider the question before imparting the following:

---

[153] While numerous surgeons use patient testimonials, the value of these testimonials to consumers are dubious, particularly for the evaluation of surgeons and surgical skill since all of the information provided is subjective , and based on the surgeon's charisma rather than skill.

- Make sure to plan to be here for an adequate time (usually ten days to weeks).
- Be sure to bring your medications and to have an adequate supply[154]. The altitude can exacerbate hypertension (high blood pressure) and this will need to be treated before any surgical procedures can be scheduled.
- Be realistic in your expectations; don't plan for more than two surgical procedures MAXIMUM. This is not "extreme makeover" and multiple surgical procedures at one time "just isn't safe." Patient safety is paramount and Dr. Pavajeau takes this rule very seriously.
- No 'tummy tuck' and abdominal liposuction at the same time, and this greatly increases the risk of pulmonary embolism, vein thrombosis and wound dehiscence.
- Diabetic patients, heart patients and people with coagulopathies need to be very careful when considering elective procedures.
- Be ready to be active, to walk after surgery, and to drink lots of fluids to prevent complications. This is very important to safeguard your health.

Dr. Pavajeau reports that he has received several awards during his career including:

- Top surgical resident for Colombia for his research on the use of silicone and comparisons in the tissue response with medical grade and construction grade silicone. However, I was unable to verify any of these awards[155].

---

[154] Thirty days worth to allow for dosing increases, if needed.

[155] Verifying awards, memberships etc. can de difficult depending on age of award and amount of cooperation of the agency, and availability of

Member of the Society of Esthetics and Plastic Surgery. Dr. Pavajeau appears to be a good surgeon; his patient unquestionably received beautiful cosmetic results after liposuction combined with fat injection. However, the procedure was performed at a small freestanding private surgical center, and during the case I observed several nonsurgical areas of concern. Of primary concern was the anesthesiologist during the case. During the case, he left the operating room for fifteen minutes. Unlike many operating rooms in the United States, anesthesia is not jointly managed by an anesthesiologist and a CRNA (certified registered nurse anesthetist.) In cases with CRNAs present, it is common for anesthesiologists to delegate care of the patient to CRNAs for much of the duration of the case. However, during this case, the patient was left unattended[156]. For part of the case, he stood in the open doorway and talked on his cellular phone. Monitors were not visible from this position. The operating room equipment was old, but it appeared well maintained and had been recently inspected[157]. The patient was poorly positioned with no head/neck support and was not secured to the operating room table[158]. The

---

computerized information. Older records as a rule are more difficult o verify, particularly awards versus certifications.

[156] As in without anesthesia monitoring of vital signs and patient condition. The surgeon was present for the duration of the case, but is busy performing surgery, and thus not able to attend to patient's other needs.

[157] Some of the equipment was vintage 1970's, including steel reusable needles for IV infusions.

[158] Patients are not always 'belted in" during surgery, but patients should be positioned to prevent injury.

patient positioning resulted in compression of the left arm for a portion of the case. This arm became mildly cyanotic in color until patient was repositioned later in the case. This also resulted in blood pressure cuff inaccuracies during the case, which were not addressed by the anesthesiologist. In fact, for several minutes the blood pressure cuff failed to cycle. (The remainder of vital signs were visible on older, but functional telemetry monitors.)

The operating room door was open and remained open to the hallway for much of the case until I physically closed it. While this door opens to a 'clean' corridor, this practice jeopardizes sterile technique and exposes the patient unnecessarily[159]. Patients and staff within the recovery room were clearly visible from the operating room through the open doorway.

Patient was equippedwith thigh high teds during the case for deep vein thrombosis prophylaxis.

Surgical Apgar score: 5

Recommended with strong reservations: Surgeon (Dr. Pavajeau) proficient, but auxiliary staff wanting. Suggest considering surgery with Dr. Pavajeau at one of the other facilities, if desired.

Dr. Claudia Turriago Prieto, MD
Email: turriageclaudia@hotmail.com

Dr. Turriago is a general surgeon who works with Dr. Pavajeau in his office, (Dr. Pavajeau is approved for

---

[159] As the patient is naked and only minimally draped, with genitalia exposed.

several in-office minor surgical procedures[160].) She specializes in hair transplant procedures.

Clinica Colombiano de Obesidad y Metobolismo
http://www.clinicacolombianaobesidad.com/
http://clinicaobesidad.com
Carrera 13 No 94A – 25
Consultorio 416
Bogota, Colombia
Tele: 622 4419
USA tele: (786) 497 8724 (Miami call center)
Email: direccioncomercial@clinicobesidad.com
Contacted via website.

The name of this clinic is misleading; Dr. Cubillos is a plastic surgeon specializing in laser surgeries. He does not perform bariatric surgery or bariatric procedures. His website lists two surgeons in this clinic, with Dr. Cubillos as director of the clinic but only Dr. Cubillos was in evidence during my onsite visit. Dr. Cubillos performs a limited range of procedures: laser facial rejuvenation, laser mastoplexy with / without breast enlargement, laser abdominal sculpting and liposuction and gluteal lifting. All of his procedures utilize lasers. The staff states he was the first doctor in Colombia to offer laser liposuction, and sells and trains other surgeons throughout South America. He and Claudia (his nurse) report that laser lipolysis liquefies fat tissue, which is then removed by using small suction catheters creating only 1 to 2 centimeter incisions,

---

[160] According to government inspection certificates.

hidden in natural skin folds. Claudia states, "It's like magic" as she shows me a large multi-page ad for the clinic in Soho magazine featuring Natalie Paris[161]. The procedures are advertised heavily as having immediate cosmetic results being virtually incision free, pain free with rapid recovery time[162]. During my initial visit, Dr. Cubillos introduced me to a patient that had the surgery a year prior. She was tall, slim and quite attractive. She did have two tiny well-healed incisions visible on her flank[163]. The patient reported that she was very satisfied with the treatment received (gluteal lift, and abdominal laser liposuction with sculpting.)

Both of these surgeons are plastic surgeons. They do offer a variety of plastic surgery procedures to remove fat via multiple liposuction therapies. They also perform the usual complement of cosmetic procedures; facial procedures, breast procedures, laser rejuvenation, cosmetic dentistry, hair transplant, etc.

They offer medical tourism packages with hotel, nurse house calls, and private car services. These services are coordinated with by Claudia Mejia Arango, (mentioned previously) who is one of the nurses in the clinic. In person, Claudia speaks passable English and was very

---

[161] Natalie Paris Gavaria is a Colombian model known primarily for her physique. The clinic reports that Ms. Paris had several procedures including laser liposuction with abdominal sculpting in addition to a gluteal lift.

[162] Natural skeptic that I am, I fairly insisted on viewing the procedure myself, but despite several requests an invitation was not forthcoming.

[163] The year-old incisions were thin lines that resembled the fingernail marks, without indentation which appear identical to healed incisions from standard liposuction.

uncomfortable discussing the surgical packages. She was able to give me a colorful brochure showing the accommodations at the hotel adjoining the separate surgery clinic and reported that the nurse makes room visits. She also gave me a copy of the English language informational materials she was currently having translated. It is noteworthy that these materials quoted a mortality risk of 10%. For people unfamiliar with surgery or statistics, bypass surgery (open heart surgery) carries a mortality risk (risk of dying) of less than 2. 5 % in most cases. While this may be an error in translation, or simply erroneous information, I caution any patient to reconsider ANY elective procedure with a quoted mortality risk approaching ten percent.

Dr. Cubillos' consultation office is in an attractive building in a nice part of town, near the French embassy. His office is relatively spacious in comparison to the often small quarters surgeons in Colombia utilize for office consultations.

Surgical procedures are performed at a separate location called La Font. This building houses the hotel, spa and the laser operating room suites on the third floor. I was unable to schedule a date to observe surgery despite multiple attempts.

Dr. Fabio Andres Mejia Ortiz, MD
http://www.doctormejia.com
Calle 98 No 9A – 46
Consultorio 502
Bogota, Colombia
Tele: 610 4814
Email: dramo@etb.net.co
Website with English version. No reply received to requests for interview.

Dr. Andre Perez Nieto, MD
www.andreperezmd.com
Carrera 7 B No. 127 A – 14
Bogota, Colombia
Tele: 258 9904
Email: drandreperez@yahoo.com

I met Dr. Perez at the Nuevo Clinica Los Cebros where he was performing a face-lift, (also with the door wide open). The patient's face was approximately 3 feet from the open door, which is a breach in sterile technique. However, his anesthesiologist appeared to be more attentive than in Dr. Pavajeau's case.

Dr. Perez trained at National University. He is a member of the Colombian Society of Plastic Surgery.

Full evaluation not performed, but I have concerns relating to facility, and facility protocols.

Dr. Martha Luz Torres Pabon, MD
Carrera 13 #144 -57
Bogota, Colombia
Tele: 274 8300
Email: mltorrespabon@yahoo.com – first email bounced; second email with no reply. Dr. Torres is a member of the Colombian Society of Plastic Surgery and is listed on the Mederi website as the Chief of the department for plastic surgery. There was no website listing found during internet searches, and the email sent to the address listed on the medical society website was returned.

Dr. Torres has no phonebook listing. Additional emails[164] were sent to attempt to contact Dr. Torres via Mederi Hospital. No response was ever received, but I met Dr. Torres in the operating room during a complex case with Dr. Lopez (thoracic surgeon). At that time, Dr. Torres was creating a muscle flap and skin graft to cover a large defect created by the removal of a large chest tumor. She took a methodical, well-planned approach to covering this large open area with skin and tissue removed from areas on the patient's stomach and thighs.

---

[164] During the research of this book, I first and foremost attempt to contact physicians using the means most convenient for international patients (i.e. email, internet first).

Vital Center Cirugia Plastica y Estetica
Dr. Jorge Andres Afanador Luque
www.vitalcenter.com.com
Calle 119 No. 14 -23 Piso 2
Bogota, Colombia
Tele. 400 6600 Calls from the USA: 305-705-7650
Email: info@vitalcenter.com

Emailed to request interview, but the email was returned as undeliverable. His official listing with the Colombian Society of Plastic Surgery gives the same address. Website has English language icon, but shows same Spanish language version. Dr. Afanador reports that he speaks English, French and Portuguese in addition to Spanish on his member listing with Colombian Society of Plastic Surgery but I was unable to confirm this.

Dr. Afanafor is a member of the Colombian Society of Plastic Surgeons and the society of Aesthetic Plastic Surgery. Dr. Afanador performs facial procedures including: face lifts, eye lifts, rhinoplasty, ear pinning, lip procedures, chin augmentation, hair transplant. Body procedures include: breast procedures, liposuction by various techniques including ultrasound, abdominal procedures including tummy tuck and gluteal augmentation.

This clinic also offers cosmetic dentistry, spa services (facial peels, cellulite treatment, rejuvenating treatments and baths), cosmetology services and a hair salon for a full range of aesthetic services. The Vital Center also offers medical tourism packages.

Association Clinica de los Andes – Spa
Dr. Carlos E. Vasquez Camargo
www.cirugiaplasticacorreccion.com
Calle 79A No. 71B – 92
Bogota, Colombia
Dr. Vasquez maintains an office for consultations at:
Diagonal 127A No. 31 -48 consultorio 417.
Bogota, Colombia
Email: info@cirugiaplasticacorreccion.com
Emailed for interview; no reply.
Website in Spanish only. In addition to the usual cosmetic procedures, Dr. Vasquez also specializes in reconstructive surgery (including post-burn surgery, hand surgery, microsurgery and genital surgery). He is a member of the Colombian Society of Maxillofacial and Hand surgery. He is also a member of international societies for microsurgery and burns and has extensive post-doctoral training in reconstructive surgery, microsurgery and hand surgery.

Dr. Gustavo Hincapie Molina
www.drgustavohincapie.com
Calle 93 No. 20 – 66
Consultorio 104
Bogota, Colombia
Tele: 479 3535
Email: ciruplastico@gmail.com
Emailed to request interview and received same day reply. Dr. Hincapie also speaks fluent English and Portuguese in addition to his native Spanish. Most of the staff primarily

speak Spanish. He is a member of the Colombian Association of Plastic Surgery, its Brazilian counterparts, as well as the International Society of Aesthetic Plastic Surgery. He trained in Colombia with specialty training in Brazil at the University of Rio Janeiro. He practiced in Brazil for several years after completing a plastic surgery fellowship there. Dr. Hincapie returned to Colombia and opened his boutique practice in 2000. He has since started a medical travel program with full service packages for international patients. He also maintains an English speaking call center located in Miami to assist North American callers. He has two aestheticists who perform many of the in-office procedures including several massage type treatments aimed at reducing cellulite[165]. He performs facial procedures such as rhinoplasty, otoplasty, mentoplasty, Co2 laser resurfacing as well as injectables. He performs breast procedures, gluteal implant/ lift procedures, abdominal sculpting and whole body liposuction. He also performs male specific procedures such as chest/ breast reduction, abdominal sculpting and penile enhancement.

All of the surgical procedures such as breast reduction and liposuction procedures are performed at independent surgical centers outside of his office; he currently operates at the Clinica del Country, the Aesthetic Medical Center, Clinica Avellanada and the New Image Clinic.

Dr. Hincapie has a "no pain after surgery program" that utilizes several techniques to reduce post-operative pain,

---

[165] There is no clinical research proving the effectiveness of these very popular treatments.

including temporary pain pumps and several treatments to reduce post-operative swelling[166]. All patients fitted with pain pumps are seen and evaluated frequently by anesthesiologists during pain pump use.

Medical travel services include several accommodation options including a family house option, in addition to hotels, as well as nursing house calls. Post-operative complication insurance is included in all medical packages[167]. Dr. Hincapie states (depending on procedure(s), that most medical stays are 1 to 3 weeks in length. Dr. Hincapie accepts some US insurances.

While the exterior of the office building is nondescript brick, the interior is attractive, modern, well-lit and very clean. Typical policies cover a two to three month period after surgery with a one million dollar limit, specifically valid in US facilities. These policies were designed with American clientele in mind to have added security after returning home.

Dr. Hincapie has an affiliation with the dental practice across the hall from his office, Clinica Estetica Dental and offers medical packages bundled with a full range of dental services.

---

[166] Several different plastic surgeons listed specialize in post-operative treatments aimed at reducing post-operative pain, and healing time.
[167] Post-operative complication insurance covers the cost of any complications developing after surgery such as infection or wound dehiscence.

Dr. Luis lberto Alvarez Pinzon
Cr 7 B No 127 A – 14
Bogota, Colombia
PBX 633 2066 telefax 633 3232
Email: md.esthetic@hotmail.com
Emailed to request interview, no reply.

Camilo Prieto, MD
www.camiloprieto.com
Cr 14A No. 112 -79
Bogota, Colombia
PBX: 213 6131
Email: atencionalpaciente@camiloprieto.com
Multiple emails to request interview; no reply. On-site visit to request interview with no response. Dr. Prieto is well-known and is heavily advertised on both the internet and in local media. For this reason, I made repeated attempts to contact Dr. Prieto and arrange for an interview, but to no avail[168].

Dr. Prieto is a local celebrity doctor with his own television show "Muy Buenos Dias" which is broadcast on RCN, a Bogota channel. His practice consists of two doctors: himself, and his colleague Dr. Carolina Granados. His clinic offers a wide range of services from facial cosmetic procedures (face lifts, eye lifts, rhinoplasty, etc) and body procedures (breast surgery, liposuction, vaginoplasty, abdominal surgery including a specialized procedure

---

[168] I called, emailed, and even visited his clinic in an attempt to arrange an interview with Dr. Prieto. I also attempted to contact him thru several other surgeons.

aimed at post-childbirth problems). Dr. Prieto's clinic is also affiliated with additional services including cosmetic dentistry, dermatology, gastroenterology, ophthalmology and otolaryngology. The clinic offers weight management services and gender specific services such as pectoral implants and hair transplants for men.

Notably, Dr. Carolina Granados specializes in reconstructive surgery particularly after trauma, burns or cancer surgery.

Dr. Nelson Chaves, MD
www.drchaves.com
Centro Medico Dali
Calle 97 No. 23 – 37
Consultorio 513 – 514
Bogota, Colombia
Tele: 642 – 1400
Email: info@drchaves.com

Contacted to request interview, physician replied in a timely fashion. He referred me to his secretary to schedule our meeting, but I had some difficulty reaching her. Doctor cancelled the first appointment well in advance of the date, and did not reschedule. I was unable to reschedule despite multiple attempts.

Member of the Colombian Society of Plastic Surgery.

Dr. Andres DeGournay
www.andresdegournay.com
Carrera 19 No. 85 -68
Consultorio 201
Bogota, Colombia
Tele: 622 – 8692

Website under construction/ not working. No email address provided.
Member of the Colombian Society of Plastic Surgery.

Dr. Yezid Masmela Diaz
www.imagenestetica.com
www.yezidmasmelacirujanoplastico.com
2 offices:

Sede Norte	**Sede Sur**
Calle 84 No. 18 -38	**Calle 16 Sur No. 20-19**
Consultorio 403	**Consultorio 204**
Tele: 618 5977	**Tele: 599 6619**

The imagen website is under construction but the other website is fully functioning, but solely in Spanish. Contacted Dr. Diaz to schedule an interview; no reply received. Not listed as a member of the Colombian Society of Plastic Surgery.

Dr. Alfredo Hoyos
http://www.alfredohoyos.com
Carrera 28 No 100 – 24
Santa Barbara Surgical Center
Bogota, Colombia
Tele: 498 – 5772
Email: info@alfredohoyo.com

Attempted to contact several times. After making the first appointment, Dr. Hoyos was detained in surgery. However, on a subsequent meeting I was able to interview Dr. Hoyo and arranged to visit him in surgery. Dr. Hoyo is apparently something of a celebrity surgeon overseas, particularly in Asia[169]. He is currently a member of the Colombian Association of Aesthetic and Plastic Surgeons but is not a member of the American Society for Aesthetic Plastic Surgery as claimed in the Spanish portion of his website1[170]. They [the American Society] reluctantly admitted to having no record of Alfredo Hoyos as a member, past or present. Membership in IPRAS, or the International Confederation of Plastic, Reconstructive and Aesthetic Surgery is confirmed by membership in Colombian Association of Aesthetic and Plastic Surgery[171].

---

[169] As was noted to me by several Korean acquaintances, who specifically asked for information about Dr. Hoyos while I was researching this project.

[170] More disturbingly, when I contacted the American Society for Aesthetic Plastic Surgery to ask if perhaps membership had lapsed, etc, I was met with a hostile response.

[171] Membership within the national (Colombia) organization confers membership in the International organization under member nations.

I attempted to contact El Rosario Universidad, where he reports he first attended medical school at the age of 15, to verify attendance but received no reply to multiple contacts.

He has a diploma from El Rosario displayed in his office with a graduation year of 1994 which supports these claims. Dr. Hoyo invented the 'high definition' liposuction techniques and travels worldwide promoting this technique which is used to fabricate the appearance of 'six pack abs' using liposuction to define underlying musculature. He reports multiple scientific articles, yet I was able to find only a single entry at Pubmed, an indexing site for medical articles. The sum total of multiple internet searches are further ads and pages by Alfredo Hoyos. He also makes substantial claims as having operated on several celebrities, including royalty, which he reports was a Saudi royal family member as well as members of a Malaysian royal family.

In person, he is very friendly and personable. Unfortunately, his operating room is plagued with many discrepancies including the problem of poor anesthesia coverage. During both cases that I witnessed, patients were allowed to remain significantly hypotensive (low blood pressure), and in one case profoundly so. While in his operating room suite, the monitors were in clear view of the surgeon, no attempt was made to address this. The anesthesiologist absented himself from the cases at various points for significant periods of time, and otherwise occupied himself at different times by sending multiple text messages, doing a crossword puzzle and reading a book to the detriment of the patients under his care. I then observed the anesthesiologist recording blood pressures in the patient's chart that were far higher than actual blood pressures. The pre-operative patient scrub was half-hearted at best, with nursing spraying a fine betadine mist on the patient, then wiping it off[172]. Due to the color (orange) of the betadine, it was visibly apparent that areas had been missed. In one case, Dr. Hoyos began his incisions prior to the betadine misting. Sterility during the cases was lax, and poorly maintained.

While surgical roles differ in Colombia from the rigidly assigned roles in the United States[173], I witnessed the surgical assistant performing much of the liposuction, and the entire breast revision procedures while Dr. Hoyos completed another portion of the liposuction procedure. Surgical assistants also performed all the closing suturing, which while technically permissible in the United States, is a poor practice in plastic surgery where the cosmetic appearance of the incision is paramount. However, I will note that the operating room door remained closed during the entire procedure which was not the case for the two surgeries adjacent to these procedures at the Santa Barbara Surgical Center. (One of these procedures was performed by Dr. Freddy Pinto, the other surgeon is unknown.)
Surgical Apgar score: 4

---

[172] Betadine is a very effective surgical scrub but it must air dry and be left on the patient for continued antiseptic action.

[173] In the United States, specially trained surgical nurses (also know as Registered Nurse First Assistants or RNFAs) can do some of the opening incisions and closing suturing. However, these nurses do not practice surgery, nor are they licensed to do so.

Not recommended for reasons stated in text.

Dr. Andres Mejia, MD
www.doctormejia.com
Calle 98 No. 9A – 46
Consultorio 502
Bogota, Colombia
Tele: 610 – 4814
Email: dramo@etb.net.co
Emailed to request interview; received timely response.
Dr. Mejia is a plastic surgeon specializing in breast procedures and rhinoplasty.

Dr. Jose Luis Pena Almario, MD
http://joseluispenalmario.com
Calle 127 No 19A -28 Consultorio 607
Bogota, Colombia
Tele: 258 0681
Email: info@joseluispenalmario.com
Email sent requesting interview.
Website is limited to one page, Spanish only.
Dr. Pena specializes in plastic surgery and reconstructive surgery. He is a member of the Society of Plastic Surgery and Esthetics, Reconstruction and the Colombian Medical College.

Dr. Freddy Pinto, MD
www.drfreddypinto.com
Santa Barbara Surgical Center
Transversal 22 No. 100 – 24
Bogota, Colombia
PBX: 257 1399
USA: (954) 775 1199
Email: drfreddypinto@drfreddypinto.com

Emailed to request interview. Dr. Pinto responded quickly to schedule an appointment, but referred me to his secretary, who was never able to make or confirm an appointment. Repeated email and telephone contact failed to yield appointment to speak with Dr. Pinto. Dr. Pinto did not acknowledge me during my visit to the Santa Barbara Surgical Center.

Website in Spanish only. Dr. Borda Freddy Alberto Pinto is a member of the Colombian Society of Plastic Surgery.

Dr. Rudolfo Reyes Abisambra, MD
http://www.reyesabisambra.com
Clinica La Sabana
Ave 19 No. 102 – 53 Consultorio 102
Bogota, Colombia
PBX: 622 1120
Email: rodoreyesabi@yahoo.com

Dr. Reyes speaks some English as well as being fluent in Portuguese and his native Spanish.

Dr. Reyes is a Brazilian trained plastic surgeon. After completing medical school (Javeriana) in 1984, Dr. Reyes completed his plastic surgery residency at Pontificia

Universidad Catolica in Rio de Janeiro, Brazil, under the tutelage of Dr. Ivo Pitanguy. He has been a board-certified, practicing plastic surgeon in Bogota since 1990. He is a member of the Colombian Society of Plastic Surgery and the Federation of Latin American Plastic Surgeons. He currently assists Dr. Ivan Santos in the operating room two days a week, in between his own cases. He performs a full range of plastic surgery procedures, but his primary specialties are mammoplasty (breast procedures), liposuction, and blapharoplasty (eyes). He also particularly enjoys reconstructive surgery, including facial reconstruction and cleft palate/ lip repairs. He performs the majority of his reconstructive cases at the Instituto Franklin Delano Roosevelt hospital. He also operates at Clinica Shaio, Clinica del Country, Clinica de Sabana and several small clinics. He usually operates solo but consults Dr. Alvaro Pendraza, MD, otolaryngologist (ENT) for particularly complex rhinoplasties such as re-operative rhinoplasties, congenital deformities and trauma cases.

In his spare time he enjoys reading historic novels, traveling, and participating in ecological preservation efforts.

During a visit to the operating room at Clinica del Country, all standard protocols were followed including pre-operative time out to confirm patient name, correct procedure, allergies and antibiotic administration. Compression devices to prevent thromboembolism, along with a heating blanket were applied. Proper patient positioning and sterile techniques were maintained

throughout the case. Dr. Reyes is deliberate, and methodical in his approach, taking special care to achieve harmonious and aesthetic results bilaterally. Nursing and operating room staff work well with Dr. Reyes.
Surgical Apgar score: 10
Highly recommended.

Dr. Felipe Roa, MD
Dr. Tito Roa, MD
http://www.drroa.com/
Unidad Medical Center – Clinica del Country
Cra 16, No. 82 – 95
Consultorio 500
Bogota, Colombia
Tele: 236 – 2135
Website in Spanish only.
This is a father and son practice. Both Drs. Roa speak Spanish. **Dr. Tito Roa** is the senior surgeon and graduated from Juan Corpus medical school in 1952. He has been operating for forty-eight years as a plastic surgeon. He laughs as he explains that over the years he has taught plastic surgery to most of the surgeons in Bogota in one of his three various professor positions. He is a three time former president of the Colombian Society for Plastic Surgery. He does not do vaser or ultrasound assisted liposuction. He also does not do fat injection as he feels this is unsafe due to the risk of pulmonary embolism[174].

---

[174] This is a hotly debated topic among plastic surgeons. A review of the current medical literature failed to reveal any conclusive link between pulmonary embolism and fat transfer (fat injection, fat grafting), but there

He does perform conventional liposuction, mammoplasty, and breast reconstruction, rhinoplasty and face-lifts. Dr. Tito Roa primarily specializes in facial procedures, while his son, Felipe Roa, usually performs the majority of body procedures in their practice.

Dr. Felipe Roa, MD has been a plastic surgeon for fourteen years. He specializes primarily in corporal (body) procedures such as liposuction, post-bariatric surgery procedures, and abdominoplasties, gluteoplasties. He also performs reconstructive surgery and enjoys performing face-lifts. He offers injectables such as Botox and dermal fillers as well.

He is a member of the Colombian Society of Plastic Surgeons, and the FILACP. He currently operates at several clinics including Clinica del Country, Clinica Café Salud VIP, Centro Medico ISKA, and Compensar. Both he and his father enforce a three - day wait for out-of-area patients. They currently do not offer any specialized services for international patients.

In the operating room, father and son both operate with a brisk, no nonsense manner. The tone of the operating room is very serious, and talk is minimal. During a portion of the case shared between both physicians, all standardized protocols were followed, compression devices applied, antibiotics received. During the liposuction portion and scar revision of the procedure performed by Dr. Felipe Roa, patient achieved good

---

were a few case reports linking large volume fat grafting with rare incidences of sepsis, abscess formation and more commonly, cosmetically undesirable results such as dimpling or pocketing of transferred fat.

cosmetic results but was noted to have a significant, but not excessive, bruising during the procedure[175]. During the rhinoplasty portion of the procedure with Dr. Tito Roa, his long experience was readily evident. He was brisk but somewhat impatient with nursing staff that were slow to respond to his needs. He quickly and efficiently performed the procedure with excellent cosmetic results with minimal bleeding. The before and after appearance of the patient within the operating room was somewhat striking; as a plain, bumpy nose that marred the patient's face was transformed into a classic, elegant nose that was in harmony with the rest of her features.

Dr. Felipe Roa: *Surgical Apgar* score: 6[176]
Dr. Tito Roa: *Surgical Apgar* score: 8
Recommended.

Dr. Freddy Sanabria, MD
http://www.sanabrialaser.com/
http://www.drsanabria.com
Carrera 7 No. 119 -14
Consultorio 310
Bogota, Colombia
Tele: 215 3666
Email: info@drsanabria.com

---

[175] This is often a normal consequence of the procedure and is both operator and patient dependent. Instillation of an epinephrine solution prior to liposuction is used to minimize bleeding and bruising but results vary.

[176] Apgar scores during liposuction procedures reflect estimated blood loss scoring since this procedure can result in significant blood loss.

Speaks excellent English, has English language version of website. His website lists him as a member of the American Society for Aesthetic Plastic Surgery[177]. He is also a member of the International Society of Plastic Surgery, and the Colombian Association of Esthetics and Plastic Surgery.

Dr. Freddy Sanabria S. comes from a family of physicians; his father, Dr. John Sanabria G. shares his plastic surgery practice, and his mother practices as a pediatric/ adult ENT specialist across the hall[178]. Dr. Sanabria has been operating for eight years since completing his training. He graduatied from Javeriana University with several visits to the United States as both a medical student (Brown, University of Pennsylvania) and as a resident (University of Pennsylvania.) He also completed a residency in Hand Surgery at Stanford, in Palo Alto, Ca. He has written several chapters in one of the primary plastic surgical textbooks used in Colombia. He is currently listed as one of the preferred providers for the American Embassy and offers surgical tourism services to his international patients including hotel, transportation, nursing services, etc.) International patients should expect to spend 10 days to one month in Bogota after surgery, depending on the procedure(s).

---

[177] A visit to their website fails to yield his name under current members with only five plastic surgeons are listed for the entire country, most located in Medellin. However, he showed a current certificate when I was in his office.

[178] She also assists with rhinoplasty cases, to restore/ maintain functionality of the nose/throat.

He offers a range of patient education materials from YouTube infomercials to more in-depth patient pre-operative teaching videos with English subtitles. His patient pre and post-operative photos were impressive with excellent cosmetic results after the initial healing period.

He also specializes in post-bariatric surgery cosmetic procedures[179]. His office includes a free-standing same day surgery center with four well equipped operating rooms and recovery areas. All of the operating rooms were large, well lit, with modern equipment. While he primarily operates in his office, he maintains privileges at both Clinica del Country and Santa Fe de Bogota. He uses pre and inter-operative checklists to ensure case standardization and reduce medical errors. He tracks his cases to identify patterns and areas of improvement[180] and reports that his rates of complications such as superficial infections falls well within the published norms.

Like many of the other plastic surgeons interviewed, Dr. Sanabria enforces a two-day wait to allow for acclimatization. He does not perform abdominal liposuction with tummy tuck procedures because of the increased risk of complications and does not perform prolonged procedures[181] or fat injections.

In the operating room, a pre-operative time out was performed, anti-embolic devices used, pre-operative

---

[179] After extensive weight loss, many patients require surgery to remove large amounts of excess skin for both health and cosmetic reasons
[180] This process is collectively called performance improvement or PI.
[181] This was defined as greater than seven hours by Dr. Sanabria.

antibiotic administered appropriately. General anesthesia was used for the case, with continuous anesthesia monitoring and appropriate hemodynamic monitoring. No intra-operative hypotension or other complications. Sterile technique was maintained throughout the case. Patient was positioned safely, with care taken to maintain airway patency. Dr. Sanabria used an areolar incision for breast augmentation, leaving minimal incisions versus an under the breast incision[182]. Dr. Sanabria uses Johnson & Johnson breast implants, which are FDA approved. He tries to minimize patient contact with latex, and latex particles, which he believes contributes to the development of capsular contracture[183]. During a second procedure[184], (face-lift), Dr. Sanabria demonstrated good surgical techniques with excellent attention to fine details with meticulous incision closure. Surgical staff were able to anticipate his needs and worked well with Dr. Sanabria.
Surgical Apgar score: 9 -10
Highly recommended.

---

[182] There are also peri-axillary and peri-umbilical approaches possible for this surgical procedure.

[183] Surgical gloves are gently rinsed with sterile saline to remove any loose powder or latex particles.

[184] Same patient.

Dr. Ivan Adolfo Santos Gutierrez, MD
http://www.ivansantos.com/
Calle 116 No. 23 – 05
Bogota, Colombia
PBX: 367 3900
Email: dirpacientes@ivansantos.com

Dr. Santos was exceedingly difficult to reach for an interview initially. However, after emailing and calling several times, I was finally able to make an appointment for an interview. I was thus, somewhat surprised at how quickly I was seen and how straight forward and pleasant Dr. Santos turned out to be. After reading about him in several local magazines[185], I expected him to be cocky or even arrogant, but he was very approachable and helpful[186]. He speaks excellent but not fluent English. Some members of his staff speak English as well.

Dr. Santos is forty-one, but he looks a decade younger. He graduated from Javeriana University, here in Bogota, seventeen years ago. He then specialized in plastic/aesthetic, maxillofacial and hand surgery, though he currently limits his practice to aesthetics. He reports that he performs more than 1200 procedures a year including 300 – 350 abdominoplasties, 300 – 350 liposuction procedures (including laser, vaser, and ultrasound

---

[185] Dr. Ivan Santos, along with Dr. Alan Gonzalez and Dr. Camilo Prieto are celebrity surgeons here in Colombia, featured in the 8 Julio 2010 issue of Jet-set, 194, pgs 56-60.

[186] If you think that surgeons present their best face to a relatively unknown nurse, like myself, you'd be sadly mistaken. Generally, what I see is a fairly accurate representation.

assisted), 200 – 250 rhinoplasties and 300 mammoplasties (breast procedures).

All of his surgeries are performed at the Shaio Clinic, and he readily invited me to observe several surgeries.

Rhinoplasty is done with local anesthesia only[187]. He uses a special device for fat injections and has performed over 6000 such injections. The breast prostheses are a German made implant, with a foam covering which is designed to reduce capsular contracture and scarring after surgery.

His clinic also offers several non-surgical options such as injectables and cellulite treatments. He offers spa services at a spa down the street from his office. Dr. Santos has created a device[188] for use during liposuction procedures that separates the fat from the fluids for subsequent fat injection[189].

Dr, Santos does offer international patient services with arrangements for medical travel. Currently, fifty percent of his patients are international patients from Texas, Florida, Brazil, and other parts of South America. He receives a large number of patients from both the Brazilian and the Swedish embassies.

His office staff coordinates medical travel arrangements including lodging, transportation, 24 hour nursing care postoperatively and other services as needed. There is a

---

[187] This limits the risk of anesthetic complications.

[188] Patent pending.

[189] Please note that patients are only injected with their own fat, obtained during that procedure.

two-day waiting period for travelers outside of the Bogota area.

Dr. Santos believes that the most important aspect of care is the patient – doctor relationship, and the quality of the surgery. While he cautions patients to be aware that the risk of possible complications exists, he has post-complication insurance for his international patients in case they develop problems once they return home.

Dr. Santos is a member of the Colombian Society for Plastic Reconstructive and Aesthetic Surgery, the International Confederation for Plastic, Reconstructive and Aesthetic Surgery, the International Society of Aesthetic Plastic Surgery, Iberolatinamerican Federal of Plastic and Reconstructive Surgery. He also volunteers with Operation Smile.

Dr. Santos often operates with a second surgeon assisting, frequently Dr. Rudolfo Reyes[190]. All of the cases witnessed were a combination of body and facial procedures. All procedures were performed under a combination of local and conscious sedation. Patients appeared comfortable during the procedures, and all standardized intra-operative protocols were followed. Sterility was maintained throughout each of the cases.

One of the cases was more complex than average; the patient was undergoing a revision after two previous surgeries several years ago (with another surgeon)[191]. In the operating room, Dr. Santos maintains remarkable

---

[190] Also profiled separately.
[191] Revisions are more difficult due to the presence of scar tissue, adhesions.

control of the room during his cases; he is able to focus on the case at hand while remaining attentive to even the smallest details[192]. Dr. Santos was meticulous in attention to detail, calm and pleasant in demeanor, and aggressive in surgical management. He has a good rapport with his OR team who were able to anticipate his needs. During one case the patient began to develop a small hematoma, which Dr. Santos promptly assessed and treated by evacuating the hematoma[193], exploring the site for further bleeding before completing surgery and transferring the patient to post-operative recovery unit. This was a relatively minor complication since Dr. Santos did exactly what should be done; however, some surgeons often delay re-exploration which may lead to the development of more serious complications. This complication was not a reflection of Dr. Santos surgical skill, but his rapid assessment and treatment is.

During his liposuction procedures, he uses a careful and gentle technique leading to minimal intra-operative bleeding, and little to no post-operative bruising visible at case conclusion[194].

During one of my visits, I met with one of Dr. Santos' American patients, a very nice Emergency Room physician from the state of New York, who had recently had surgery. She had nothing but praise for Dr. Santos and was very

---

[192] In comparison, some surgeons are so intently focused during their cases that they turn out all external stimuli such as hemodynamic monitors, and other non-operative issues.

[193] A collection of blood within the tissues, similar to a bruise.

[194] In fact, out of all of the physicians observed, Dr. Santos consistently had the least bleeding or bruising following liposuction procedures.

pleased by her care and results. In addition, during a subsequent interview with Dr. Reyes, Dr. Reyes reported, "I taught Ivan, but now, he teaches me. He is probably the best surgeon in Colombia, and the best [surgeon] for rhinoplasty."

Surgical Apgar scores: 9 -10, consistently

Highly recommended. Excellent surgeon with outstanding results.

Bogota Plastic Surgery Center
Dr. Pedro Antonio Urazan Pena
www.bogotaplastic.com
Calle 93 No. 19 – 58
Bogota, Colombia
Tele: 475 9144
Email: urazanestetica@yahoo.com or
Bogota_plastic_surgery@hotmail.com

Website currently under construction.

Dr. Urazan, his associate, Dr. Zamora and his entire office staff were exceeding gracious and friendly during my unscheduled and unannounced visit to his clinic. Dr. Urazan speaks passable English, and Dr. Zamora speaks excellent English. Dr. Urazan is a member of the Colombian Society of Plastic Surgery. Dr. Urazon has 25 years experience in plastic surgery and reports that he has operated on over 50,000 patients.

He has a free standing operating room and recovery area within clinic grounds. The rooms were being repainted during my visit, but all of the surgical equipment and monitoring devices appear dated but modern and well maintained[195]. The treatment and operating rooms were small and opened directly to an open-air courtyard[196]. He has a spa attached to the clinic and offers aesthetic services as well (sauna, massage, ultrasound therapies, etc.). He has two medical doctors[197], a husband and wife team (Dr. Jorge Enrique Zamora and Dr. Luz Helena Urazon Prieto[198]) that oversee and assist with post-operative care. Dr. Urazon also has an anesthesiologist on staff. He reports that less than five percent of surgeries in his clinic require general anesthesia. The majority of surgeries utilize a combination of conscious sedation and local analgesia or regional blocks.

Dr. Urazan has medical travel packages; and he prides himself on patient-specific personalized programs and personal attention to each patient. Patients are offered the option of a clinic owned house for their comfort or nearby hotels. Patients have daily post-operative visits and house calls, if needed. Prior to surgery, patients receive sightseeing tours while they become accustomed to the increased altitude. Most travel visits are 2 to 3 weeks in duration, and packages include post-operative complication insurance. He also has arrangements and

---

[195] Equipment appeared to be approximately ten years old, but not ancient.
[196] Theoretically, this may increase potential chance of infection. However if all incisions are covered prior to leaving the operating room suite, this is unlikely.

[197] Doctors specializing in internal medicine, not surgery.
[198] Dr. Helena Urazon, his niece, also works in the Emergency department of Clinica de la Mujer.

admitting privileges with local hospitals for in-patient stays, if necessary. His clinic is modest but clean.

Dr. Alan Gonzalez Valena, MD
www.alangonzalez.com
Carrera 13 93 – 68
Consultorio 403
Bogota, Colombia
Tele: 662 – 4123
Email: ag@alangonzalez.com

Attempted to contact several times; no reply. Dr. Gonzalez is heavily advertised and is one of three 'celebrity' plastic surgeons well-known through out Bogota and Colombia for their services. However despite multiple phone calls, I was unable to speak to Dr. Gonzalez. All of my emails went unanswered, and the security at his building forbids unscheduled visits.

Selected Providers in Other Surgical Specialties

Dr. German De La Hoz, MD
Maxilofacial Surgeon
Email: german.delahoz@gmail.com

Dr. De La Hoz speaks fair English. He is an ENT, oral and maxillofacial surgeon. He performs plastic and reconstructive procedures, oncologic procedures, dental surgery, and trauma surgery on the soft tissues of the head and neck. He has been a professor of head and neck surgery for over fifteen years.

He has operating privileges at Clinica de la Mujer, Clinica Marly, Clinica del Country, and Nuevo Clinica. He takes emergency calls in the ER at Clinica de la Mujer daily.

In his spare time he enjoys diving, fishing and tennis. He speaks a little Arabic, a little French and continues to study and improve his English.

Ophthalmology
Dr. Mario Guillermo Serrano Mendez, MD
http://www.ojos-innovision.com/
Calle 113 No 7 – 45 Torre B
Consultorio 718
Bogota, Colombia
Tele: 637 – 5003
Email: innovision.info@gmail.com

Website in Spanish only, but promises a response to all emails within 24 hours.

Dr. Serrano is locally known for operating on the President of Colombia, Juan Manual Santos. Dr. Serrano performs a full range of ophthalmology treatments including cataract surgery, corneal transplant, laser vision correction and radio keratoplasty, as well as medical treatment of other vision and eye disorders.

Vascular Surgery

Dr. Heinz George Hiller Correa
Email: hhiller@cardioinfantil.org
Attempted to contact several times for interview, but received no reply.
Not listed as a member of the Colombian Society of Vascular Surgery. Listed as a practicing physician under Telemedicina Vascular.com (TMV); see below for further information.

Dr. Jorge Emilio Navarro Sanchez, MD
http://www.clinicavascular.ws/cms/default
Clinica Vascular de Colombia
Email: navarror@cable.net.co
Emailed to request interview, no reply received.

Telemedicina Vascular (TMV)
http://www.telemedicinavascular.com
This is a remote / telemedicine consultation service based in Bogota. After being unsuccessful in contacting several vascular surgeons in Bogota using other contact information, I attempted to contact these surgeons via the TMV on-line contact form but received no reply. The website is set up to allow for remote diagnosis using

patient submitted diagnostics such as arterial duplex studies for physician interpretation and diagnosis. This service is affiliated with Fundacion Vascular.

Dr. Ricardo Renteria
Vascular and Thoracic Surgeon

Please see profile under thoracic surgery for more information. However, as a vascular surgeon, Dr. Renteria primarily treats venous disease (venous insufficiency, varicose veins) versus arterial disease (aneurysms, peripheral arterial disease).

Cardiothoracic Surgery

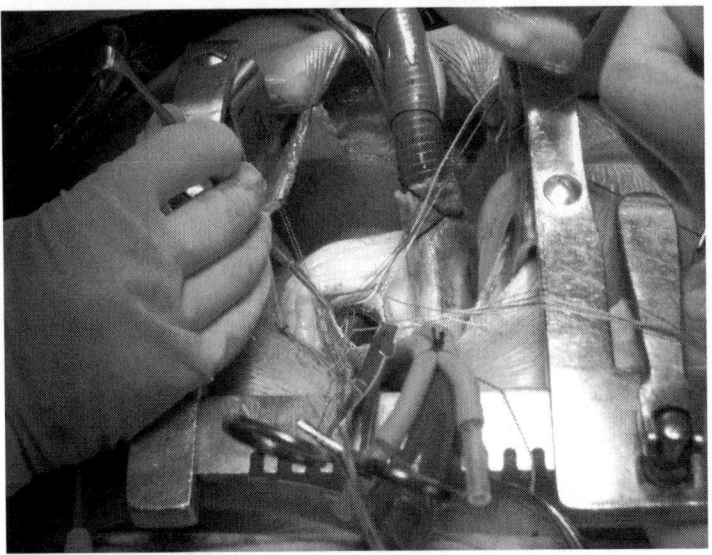

Aortic Valve Replacement

While it may surprise many people, cardiac surgery, not plastic surgery is the number one surgical specialty outsourced to medical tourism. While hard data on the numbers of people seeking cardiac surgery overseas is difficult to come by, impending shortages in cardiothoracic surgeons will only increase demand for cardiac surgery outside of the United States. The number of current practicing surgeons, with a median age of 56, and high vacancy rates coupled with the projected doubling of demand by 2030[199], make the need to identify suitable providers outside of North America a critical imperative[200].

In comparison to several other countries, Colombia's surgeons and training programs for cardiac and thoracic surgery provide the greatest approximation to American training. Cardiac and thoracic surgery in Colombia are split into two separate specialties; both specialties include general surgery residency as part of the required training, which is not the case in many other countries[201]. Notably, one significant difference that does exist is the delegation of esophageal surgery to general surgeons. In this instance, particularly in regards to patients with esophageal cancer, I strongly recommend pursuing surgery at an esophageal cancer treatment center in the United States, with an American board-certified thoracic surgeon. This is critical for this surgery due to the high risk of morbidity and mortality when this procedure is performed by general surgeons or in low-volume centers. Studies suggest a surgeon needs to perform approximately 25 cases per year to retain competency.

---

[199] Williams, T. E., Sun, B., Ross, P., & A. M. Thomas. (2010). A formidable task: Population analysis predicts a deficit of 2000 cardiothoracic surgeons by 2030. J. Thorac Surg 2010 Apr; 139 (4); 835-40..

[200] Grover et. al. (2009) predicts this shortage will occur more rapidly, in less than a decade. Grover, A. et. al. (2009). Shortage of cardiothoracic surgeons' likely by2020. Circulation, 2009; 120; 488-494.

[201] Wood, D. E. & Farjah, F. (2009). Global differences in the training, practice, and interrelationship of cardiac and thoracic surgeons. Ann Thorac Surg. 2009 Aug; 88 (2); 515 – 21.

As mentioned above, in Colombia, cardiothoracic surgery is separated into two distinct and separate specialties; Cardiac surgery encompasses multiple heart procedures including bypass surgery, valve surgery, anti-arrhythmia procedures, and repair of the great vessels such as thoracic aneurysm repair.

In patients with stable cardiac disease[202], travel is usually safe and reasonable. Given the cost of heart surgery, which often exceeds 100,000 dollars in the United States, more and more uninsured and underinsured patients are looking for alternative options such as Colombia. On average, most heart surgeries (bypass) cost around $12,000 in Colombia including surgery, ICU stay and most treatments during hospitalization. (These costs may change.)

In Bogota there are several excellent cardiac surgery programs. These programs are listed below, by hospital, alphabetically.

The thoracic surgery specialty is equally important[203], and includes multiple lung procedures such as lung resection for lung cancers, treatment of other pulmonary conditions such as empyema, pneumothorax, and pleural effusion. Thoracic surgery also includes all non-cardiac procedures involving the chest such as diseases and conditions of the

---

[202] This includes asymptomatic patients, and patients with stable angina which is easily controlled with medications.

[203] This is due to impending shortages caused by advanced age of existing US surgeons, and vacancies in existing training programs. Also, many cardiothoracic surgeons in the US elect not to practice thoracic surgery.

diaphragm, esophagus and chest wall[204]. In modern medicine many of the thoracic procedures can be performed by VATs (video-assisted thoracoscopy) resulting in smaller incisions, faster healing and less pain for the patient versus traditional open incisions. However, some thoracic procedures including very large chest tumors such as thymomas may require a larger incision for removal.

Currently, the only thoracic surgery training program in Colombia is located in Bogota at the University El Bosque, but several excellent surgeons are in the local area. Surgery can sometimes be challenging in patients with poor lung function at the increased altitude[205], but this is often the norm in thoracic surgery. Further discussion of the thoracic surgery specialty is included under the separate thoracic surgery heading, including information about pre-operative optimization.

Note: Surgical Apgar scores are not applicable for cardiac procedures due to the nature of the surgeries, and cardiac surgeries have not been rated using this tool.

---

[204] For all patients seeking thoracic surgery, it is important to verify that the surgeon is a board certified thoracic surgeon. In many facilities, particularly smaller hospitals in the United States, these procedures are often performed by general surgeons with no specialty training in thoracics which may lead to an increased incidence of complications. All of the doctors listed here are specialty trained in thoracic surgery.

[205] This is usually a problem for oxygen dependent individuals but may be addressed pre-operatively thru Pulmonary Rehabilitation.

Clinica SaludCoop

The SaludCoop program is smaller than Cardioinfantil or Clinica Shaio, but the two surgeons manage to maintain a respectably high surgical volume. However, the perfusionist at this facility does not have a cellsaver[206]. Both surgeons, Dr. Jimenez and Dr. Rincon speak English.

Dr. Mauricio Armando Jimenez Chaura
SaludCoop 104
Autopiso Norte 104 – 33
Bogota, Colombia
Email: maojim@yahoo.com

(Not to be confused with Dr. Mauricio Jimenez, plastic surgeon.) Dr. Jimenez replied quickly to initial email to schedule an interview. He is a member of CTSnet.org, the Latin American Society for Cardiovascular and Thoracic Surgery. Dr. Jimenez is also featured on a medical equipment website discussing the use of surgical hemostasis products, at www.gelilmedical.com.

Dr. Jimenez operates in SaludCoop 104.

He performs bypass surgery, valve replacement, Bentall procedures, minimally invasive valve replacement as well as endovascular procedures such as endovascular aneurysm repair (EVAR) and transcutaneous valve procedures (TAVI). After becoming a cardiac surgeon, Dr. Jimenez received additional endovascular training in Europe. He has done seven transcutanous aortic valve

---

[206] A device used during surgery to collect, clean and recycle blood shed during operations for autotransfusion. This device helps limit the amount of blood products patients receive after surgery.

procedures so far[207]. He reports that none of his patients have had serious infections (mediastinitis, sepsis) in the last three years. Dr. Jimenez along with his colleague, Dr. Rincon, perform approximately 300 surgeries a year.

Dr. Jimenez does not use a cellsaver during the majority of his cases, but does autotransfuse shed blood back to patients during surgery to minimize intra-operative blood loss. There was no intra-operative transeophageal echocardiography or cerebral oximetry[208]. There did not appear to be a regulated patient cooling mechanism during the case (i.e. cooling blanket) outside of ambient temperature regulation[209], but the patient stayed within an acceptable range.

Dr. Jimenez harvested the saphenous vein using a skip harvest technique with two small 3cm incisions. Glucose monitoring was performed periodically during the case as a part of grouped labs, and no major fluxuations were noted during surgery[210]. Hemodynamics remained stable pre and post cardiopulmonary bypass with acceptable use of vasopressors[211].

Recommended with reservations: Dr. Jimenez is a talented heart surgeon with excellent patient outcomes but lack of a

---

[207] At the time of my initial interview with Dr. Jimenez in February 2011.

[208] Please note that the utility of cerebral oximetry monitoring is widely debated.

[209] The operating room thermostat, was kept in the 60's during the case (standard for cardiac ORs).

[210] The highest glucose during the procedure was 126.

[211] Medications used to change cardiac output, raise blood pressure.

cellsaver and TEE intra-operatively make it difficult to recommend without reservation.

Dr. Jose Rincon

Dr. Rincon also operates at SaludCoop with Dr. Jimenez. There was no opportunity to observe surgery with Dr. Rincon as primary surgeon.

Clinica Shaio
Diag 115 A No. 70 C – 75
Bogota, Colombia
Tele: 617 8252

Clinica Shaio was the first hospital to perform cardiac surgery in Bogota and has several banners advertising its historic origins. The surgeons at Clinica Shaio first began performing heart surgery in 1964[212], and the heart surgery program remains a cornerstone of Clinica Shaio today, with five full-time cardiac surgeons on staff.

Clinica Shaio also has the distinction of recently operating on the Vice-President of Colombia, Angelino Garzon[213]. According to Dr. Andrade, the Clinica Shaio continues to

---

[212] While there are historical accounts of isolated heart surgery cases as far back as the 1890's, modern heart surgery (on a large scale versus isolated cases) did not develop until the development of extracorporal circulation. The Mayo Clinic was one of the earlier American heart surgery programs, and it opened March 15, 1955. From Stephenson, W. L. (2003). History of cardiac surgery. In Cohn LH, Edmunds LH Jr, eds. Cardiac Surgery in the Adult. New York: McGraw-Hill, 2003:3-29.

[213] Angelino Garzon, New Colombia VP, has heart surgery after 2 days on job. The Huffington Post, (2010, Aug. 9).

maintain high surgical volumes[214] and provides more surgical interventions that any other facility in Bogota.

Dr. Hernando Santos Calderon, MD
Av Suba, 104 – 50
Bogota, Colombia
Tele: 271 0600
No email address provided.

Dr. Santos is the chief of cardiac surgery at Clinica Shaio. He is also cousin to the President of Colombia, Juan Manual Santos, and operated on the vice-president of Colombia, as mentioned above. Despite being featured frequently in *Bogota Jet-Set* social pages and being the chief of a prestigious cardiac surgery program, Dr. Santos remains refreshingly low key and down to earth. "I'm not Chief of surgery; we're just a bunch of friends."

Dr. Santos trained at Shaio in 1979 and has been operating at Clinica Shaio since 1982. He completed a year of fellowship under Dr. Pierre Gordon in Miami and reports that he performs approximately 200 to 250 cases per year. At Shaio, Dr. Santos maintains the cardiac surgery program as a teaching service, with one cardiac surgery resident each year, which is shared with San Ignacio. There are also several general surgery residents that rotate through, along with anesthesia residents.

While Dr. Santos is certainly a genial enough and talented surgeon, I have some reservations about the operating

---

[214] 800 – 1000 cardiac surgery procedures per year, according to Dr. Andrade. The Chief of cardiac surgery revises this estimate to 800 cases per year.

room procedures at Clinica Shaio. I observed an Aortic Valve Replacement procedure with Dr. Hernando Santos. Preprocedural standards and protocols were followed with special attention paid to sterility since this was an infective endocarditis case; all personnel, myself included, wore disposable scrubs, and antibiotics were administered according to current recommendations. Pre-operative echocardiograms were reviewed intra-operatively. Anesthesia was consistent and continuous with an anesthesia team, led by an attending anesthesiologist. Dr. Santos' surgical skills are without reproach, but there was neither cellsaver, nor tranesophageal echocardiogram (TEE) utilized during this case[215]. I was told that the one existing TEE probe was being used in a case next door (there were three cases simultaneously that morning). I find the lack of available equipment disheartening at a 'heart hospital.' On subsequent visits the patient was noted to be doing well.

Recommend with reservations: Technically proficient but lack of proper equipment discouraging.

Dr. Dario Andrade, MD
Diagonal 115a No. 70c-75
Bogota, Colombia
Tele: 6178252
Email: danadradef@hotmail.com

---

[215] Use of intra-operative TEE is particularly important during valve replacement cases to monitor the function of the newly implanted valve prior to chest closure.

Dr. Andrade responded quickly to an email requesting an interview. Member of CTSnet.org. He readily gave a tour of the facility and answered all questions.

Dr. Andrade is the most recent surgeon to join the cardiac surgery department at Clinica Shaio. He reports that he is also one of two surgeons at Clinica Shaio to offer and embrace minimally invasive cardiac surgery.

Dr. Andrade did not respond to requests to visit the operating room.

Dr. Victor Caicedo
Avenida 54, No.104-50
Consultorio No. 7
Bogota, Colombia
Tele: 271-5640
Email: victorcaicedo23@hotmail.com

Dr. Caicedo never responded to multiple emails, even after meeting him at Clinica Shaio. Dr. Caicedo has been operating at Clinica Shaio for over twenty years and is well-respected in the local cardiac surgery community. Member of CTSnet.org, the Latin American Society for Cardiovascular and Thoracic Surgery.

Fundacion Cardioinfantil
Instituto de Cardiologia
Calle 163 No 28 – 60, piso 3
Bogota, Colombia
Tele: 517 679 0663

The cardiovascular and aortic surgery program at Cardioinfantil is widely acknowledged as one of the premiere cardiac surgery programs in Bogota[216] and all of Colombia.

This program is also widely known for its pediatric cardiac surgery program, headed by Dr. Nestor Sandoval. Cardioinfantil initiated a cardiac surgery training program (residency) in 2000 and, following success in that area, expanded with a vascular surgery training program in 2006. One of the criticisms of this program is that the very success that led to wide-spread expansion has also caused the program to be more impersonal[217].

Dr. Juan Pablo Unama Mallarino, MD
Fundacion Cardioinfantil, Instituto de Cardiologia
Calle 163 No 28 – 60, piso 3
Bogota, Colombia
Tele: 679 0663
Email: jpumana@yahoo.com

---

[216] Among Bogota residents, opinions are somewhat split between residents recommending Clinica Shaio and the newer program at Cardioinfantil.

[217] One surgeon commented, "It's too American – the doctors don't spend as much time with their patients." Of note, these criticisms were presented by surgeons in direct competition with Cardioinfantil.

Member of CTSnet.org, the Latin American Society for Cardiovascular and Thoracic Surgery.

Dr. Juan Pablo Umana is the chief of the adult cardiac surgery program. Trained at Stanford, he is a charismatic and engaging individual. He speaks excellent English. Both he and Dr. Sandoval strive to make Fundacion Cardioinfantil competitive with, and on par with, facilities world-wide.

Under Dr. Umana's direction, the program has already begun performing transcutaneous valve replacement, and had performed more than a dozen cases at the time of my initial interview with Dr. Umana. In fact, Dr. Umana was on the forefront of percutaneous valve technology development. Together with Dr. Mehmet Oz, at Columbia University, he developed the first percutaneous mitral clip[218]. He has had multiple publications on the treatment of mitral valve disease, thoracic aneurysms/ dissections and other cardiovascular topics[219].

In the operating room, all standardized protocols were followed; transesophageal echocardiography (TEE) was appropriately utilized, with excellent anesthesia and perfusion coverage. The patient was managed within acceptable hemodynamic parameters[220]. Serial glucose

---

[218] Dr. Umana and Dr. Oz received patent number 6269819 for this device in August 2001.

[219] Dr. Umana also had several published research articles for animal studies and liver disease.

[220] Due to use of cardiopulmonary bypass (CPB), these parameters differ from standard cases (i.e. no heart rate during CPB/ arrest).

monitoring, (patient euglycemic during the duration of the case.) Cellsaver used for autotransfusion.

Dr. Umana was focused and meticulous during the case, which was a complex combination mitral valve / bypass graft case.

Highly recommended. World class surgeon, operating at an excellent facility.

Dr. Juan Pablo Umana, author, Dr. Nestor Sandoval

Dr. Jaime Camacho, MD
Fundacion Cardioinfantil, Division Cirugia
Cardiovascular
Calle 163 No 13 B - 60
Bogota, Colombia
Tele: 679 0663
Email: jcamacho@yahoo.com

Member of CTSnet.org, the Latin American Society for Cardiovascular and Thoracic Surgery, the Colombian Society of Vascular Surgery.

Dr. Camacho specializes in surgery of the great vessels; aneurysm repair of the thoracic and abdominal aorta utilizing both hybrid and endovascular techniques. Dr. Camacho is a soft-spoken, kind individual who is trained in both vascular and cardiac surgery[221]. His retiring manner and modesty during our interview belies his skill set. He became a vascular surgeon first, after completing a fellowship in New Jersey in 1995. After practicing for five years, Dr. Camacho began additional training to become a cardiothoracic surgeon and completed residencies in Houston, Texas and Stanford, in Palo Alto, California. He began working at Cardioinfantil in 2002 and began performing hybrid procedures in 2005[222].

---

[221] Dr. Camacho attended an abridged cardiac and vascular surgery training program in comparison to traditional training which is: 5 years general, 2-3 years cardiac, and 2 years vascular. He completed four years general surgery with 2 years additional specialty training. This is common practice for practicing surgeons who want to expand their skill set.

[222] Hybrid procedures combine endovascular techniques with open surgery for repair of complex conditions.

He is an integral part of the multidisciplinary team that evaluates patients preoperatively to determine the appropriate treatment regimen; surgery, endovascular, or medical management[223]. He continues to perform a wide range of procedures utilizing his dual training: aneurysms, dissections, coronary bypass and valve procedures along with peripheral vascular procedures such as aortio-femoral bypass, femoral-popliteal bypass.

At the Aortic clinic, Dr. Camacho and his colleagues treat patients with systems approach versus body part[224]203; they treat all vascular disease from the aortic valve and the great vessels to the iliacs.

Pediatric Cardiac Surgery – at Cardioinfantil
In addition to performing pediatric cardiac surgery, both Dr. Sandoval and Dr. Bresciano operate on adults[225].
Dr. Nestor Sandoval, MD
Fundacion Cardioinfantil, Instituto de Cardiologia
Calle 163 No 28 – 60, piso 3
Bogota, Colombia
Tele: 517 679 0663
Email: nestorsandoval@cable.net.co
Dr. Sandoval replied quickly to email to arrange initial interview. He is a member of CTSnet.org, the Latin

---

[223] This approach is much more evidence-based and protects the patient from doctor/ treatment bias by obtaining input from multiple specialties.
[224] Many programs stratify patients by location; patients see a cardiac surgeon for aortic disease in the chest, and a vascular surgeon for disease below the diaphragm.
[225] Dr. Sandoval operated on the grandmother of one of the families I stayed with in Bogota over ten years ago. She remains healthy and active.

American Society for Cardiovascular and Thoracic Surgery.

Nestor Sandoval is essentially the father of modern pediatric heart surgery in Bogota. He is well-known by the majority of Bogota residents[226]. Surprisingly, despite widespread fame throughout Colombia, Dr. Sandoval is an exceedingly modest, soft-spoken gentleman. Despite his long and illustrious career in the operating room, Dr. Sandoval remains a fit and attractive man in his early fifties[227]. He worked at Clinica Shaio, which was the first heart hospital in Bogota for twenty years before coming to Fundacion Cardioinfantil.

Dr. Sandoval genuinely cares for his patients and their families, and spends a generous amount of his time explaining procedures and treatments to the families of his patients. In the operating room all standardized protocols were followed, strict aseptic technique used, state-of-art equipment, with well trained operating room personnel. Two surgeons as is standard in Colombia[228].

In his spare time he enjoys spending time with his extended family and has been learning to play the saxophone.

---

[226] In fact one of the taxi cab drivers regaled me with stories about his daughter and her life saving heart surgery as an infant. The daughter is now grown and a mother herself. These stories are a common thread during my stay in Bogota.

[227] After hearing all the stories about Dr. Sandoval from other members of the cardiology and cardiac surgery community, I expected someone much older, elderly statesman-like..

[228] This is also standard procedure at some, but not all American facilities.

Highly recommended, in fact, the entire cardiac surgery program at Cardioinfantil exceeds all expectations.

Dr. Sandoval with one of his pediatric patients after surgery[229]

Dr. Renato Bresciano, MD
Fundacion Cardioinfantil, Instituto de Cardiologia
Calle 163 No 28 – 60, piso 3
Bogota, Colombia

---

[229] Notably, the patient pictured above underwent an exceedingly complex surgery for repair of congenital malformations (which I witnessed). This photo was taken three days after surgery, as the patient was playing in the children's play area in the cardiac center.

Tele: 517 679 0663

Dr. Bresciano also trained at the University of Alabama[230],Birmingham with Dr. Nestor Sandoval. When Dr. Bresciano isn't operating at Fundacion Cardioinfantil, he flies to another facility outside of Bogota to operate in Buscaramanga two days a month (or approximately 70 surgeries a year). He shrugs when discussing his role in providing life-saving surgery for pediatric patients who are unable to come to Bogota. Like Dr. Sandoval, he is an unassuming, modest man who downplays his importance and role within the pediatric surgery program. He is jovial, friendly and engaging.

During my visits to Cardioinfantil, Dr. Bresciano also performed several high complexity cases on neonates. Both Dr. Sandoval and Dr. Bresciano also perform cardiac surgery procedures on adults.

Fundacion Santa Fe de Bogota

The cardiac surgery program at Fundacion Santa Fe de Bogota is more modest in scale when compared with either Clinica Shaio or Cardioinfantil. There is no pediatric cardiac surgery division[231].

---

[230] The international cardiac surgery community is fairly small. I was lucky enough to have worked for a wonderful surgeon at Duke, Dr. Richard Embrey, who was a classmate to both Drs. Sandoval and Bresciano during their shared fellowship at the University of Alabama – Birmingham.

[231] Pediatric cardiac surgery is not an essential service for most hospitals. In fact, there are fewer than 100 hospitals offering pediatric cardiac surgery services in the United States.

Dr. Javier Dario Maldonado Escalante, MD
Calle 22 B No. 66 – 46
Consultorio 919
Bogota, Colombia
Tele: 594 8650
Email: javierdm@cable.net.co
javierdmaldonado@gmail.com

Spoke with Dr. Maldonado[232] briefly during a chance encounter at Clinica Colombia while interviewing another surgeon. At that time we exchanged emails, he readily scheduled an interview and observation of surgery. He speaks English, Portugeuse and Spanish. Dr. Maldonado is featured on two different medical tourism websites (SURE[233], Clinica Colsanitas medical tourism program[234]), but does not have a private website. He is a member of CTSnet.org, the Latin American Society for Cardiovascular and Thoracic Surgery. He currently operates at Clinica Colombia, Clinica de Marly and Fundacion Santa Fe de Bogota, as the Chief of Cardiac Surgery, along with another surgeon, Dr. Fernando Diaz Yamal. Dr. Maldonado reports that between these facilities his cardiac service line is performing almost 700

---

[232] There is another well-known Dr. Javier Maldonado in Colombia, a primary care physician who works with the indigenous tribes in the Amazon.

[233] Dr. Maldonado's online profile can be found here: http://www.suremedicaltourism.com/ing/procedures/heart_surgery/index_heart_surgery.html.

[234] http://www.clinicacolsanitas.com/ - under cardiovascular surgery.

cases per year[235]. Dr. Maldonado prides himself on the personalized care he provides. Along with the assistance of two nurses, Norma and Sandra, Dr. Maldonado reports that he sees his patients regularly, before and after surgery[236]. Dr. Maldonado also has a growing surgical treatment program for atrial fibrillation. He reports that growth of the program has been slow due to a lack of outside referrals, but that his program is coordinated with several cardiologists at Clinica Colombia including electrophysiologists. Dr. Maldonado reports that he hopes to start a transplant program in the near future but is waiting for government approval.

Dr. Maldonado also reports that approximately 90% of his cardiac bypass cases are performed without cardiac pulmonary bypass (i.e. offpump[237]).

In the operating room (at Clinica Colombia), all protocols and procedures were followed in accordance to international standards. Since the case was "off-pump," the perfusionist stood by, as usual precaution in the event that conversion to CPB is needed. Continuous anesthesia monitoring, but no TEE used[238]. Sterility maintained throughout the surgery. Dr. Maldonado was assisted by

---

[235] This is considered a busy service line. The average heart surgeon performs around 200 cardiac surgeries a year.

[236] In the USA, and other countries, patients are often primarily cared for by residents, nurse practitioners/ physician assistants and interns after surgery in large institutions.

[237] Cardiopulmonary bypass (CPB) or the heart-lung machine is not used. This technique became popular in the late 1990's and has distinct advantages and disadvantages over traditional surgery.

[238] Pembrook, L. (2006, Nov). TEE uncovers cardiac pathology, guides central line placement. Clinical Anesthesiology; 32:11.

Dr. Arrieta during the case. Dr. Maldonado was calm, proficient and the case proceeded without significant hypotension or hemodynamic compromise. There were no intra-operative complications.
Highly recommended.

Dr. Jorge Fernando Vargas Velez, MD
Email: fevave@hotmail.com
Email sent to request interview.
Not listed on CTSnet.org

Hospital Universitario San Ignacio
Dr. Juan Rafael Correa Ortez, MD
Carrera 7A # 40 – 62 Consultorio 723
Bogota, Colombia
Tele: 287 4393
Email: jrcorrea@javeriana.edu.co
Emailed to interview request, and received reply quickly to schedule an interview. Dr. Correa is a member of CTSnet.org, the Latin American Society for Cardiovascular and Thoracic Surgery.

Dr. Correa speaks fluent English. He completed much of his training in the United States including stints at Oregon Health Sciences program and University of Alabama at Huntsville. Unfortunately, the cardiac surgery program at San Ignacio appears to by limping along, with low overall surgical volumes for the two cardiac surgeons, and a vascular surgeon. San Ignacio has a shared surgical residency program[239]. The program averages about twenty cardiac cases a month, barely enough to sustain the existing program, which includes pediatric cases, transplant and endovascular services. In a city filled with excellent cardiovascular surgery options, this program has been easily overlooked.

Instituto Cardiologia San Rafael
www.cardiosanrafael.com
Carrera 8A No 17 – 45 Sur
Bogota, Colombia
PBX 328 2300

The Institute Cardiologia San Rafael has a moderate sized cardiac surgery program with three cardiac surgeons, and three perfusionists. The institute also provides cardiac surgery coverage to Mederi and Colsubsido as an outsourced service.

The program is struggling in many ways; despite having an adequate case volume of 400 – 500 per year; the website for cardiothoracic surgery, for example, hasn't been updated in several years, and the surgeons appear to have little administrative support. The Mederi arm of the cardiac surgery program is particularly disappointing; surgical outcomes fall far short of expectations with an admitted mortality of 11%[240]. This is far greater than expected and represents a failure in post-operative

---

[239] The surgical residency slot is shared with Clinica Shaio, with the resident alternating years between each clinic.

[240] Typical mortality for cardiac surgery overall is 2.0 – 2.5 %.

management and a lack of continuity of care brought on by rotating surgical coverage and outsourcing of care to noncardiac surgery physicians and residents[241]. *Until aggressive steps are taken to correct these deficiencies, patients are advised to avoid this program (Mederi).*

Dr. Pablo Antonio Guerra, MD
Email: pablogl@yahoo.com
No reply to emails. Member of CTSnet.org, the Latin American Society for Cardiovascular and Thoracic Surgery. Dr. Guerra performs adult cardiac surgery only.

Dr. Diego German Pineros, MD
Email: diegopineros@yahoo.com
Emailed with timely reply received; initial interview at Clinica Infantil Colsubsido, with subsequent interviews at Clinica San Rafael.
Dr. Pineros speaks excellent English.
Member of CTSnet.org, the Latin American Society for Cardiovascular and Thoracic Surgery. Dr. Pineros, along with Drs. Guerra and Velez, works at San Rafael, Hospital Mayor, and Mederi. They also rotate to San Juan de Dios in Cartagena to supplement services there with Dr. Fernandez. He and Dr. Velez also perform scheduled pediatric cardiac surgery one day a week[242] at Clinical Infantil Colsubsido. He operates three days a week at San Rafael. Dr. Pinero is a very friendly and approachable. He

---

[241] Thank you to staff and physicians at Mederi for being forthcoming about program shortcomings during interviews.

[242] Dr. Pinero and Dr. Velez also perform emergency cases as needed.

has worked at San Rafael since 2006. Prior to that, he worked at Fundacion CardioInfantil with Dr. Bresciani, Dr. Camacho, Dr. Naldonado and Dr. Velez, after completion of his cardiac surgery training in 1996. Like many of the surgeons I have met during my research here in Bogota, Dr. Pineros takes his commitment to the community and his patients very seriously. During one of my visits to Clinica San Rafael, Dr. Pineros was organizing a trip to a smaller city, three hundred miles outside of Bogota, to perform pediatric heart surgery at a rural hospital that is otherwise without pediatric cardiac services. When asked about the trip, Dr. Pineros shrugged and stated, "It would be impossible for these patients and their families to come to Bogota for surgery. Many of these patients have already come long distances to get to the hospital at Tolima. So we will fly down there this weekend, and stay until the patients recover." This is apparently, how Dr. Pineros spends his 'leisure time', before returning to a full surgical schedule back in Bogota. In the operating room, Dr. Pineros is calm, relaxed but focused. Prior to the initial incision, a time-out was performed with patient identification confirmation, antibiotic administration, etc.. All pre-operative procedures and protocols were followed. The patient remained hemodynamically stable throughout the case with continuous anesthesia monitoring. The case proceeded quickly, with no intra-operative complications. The patient was subsequently discharged home the same day.

One of the other cases I was scheduled to see was cancelled because on arrival to the pre-operative area, the patient was noted to be wheezing heavily. At that time, he received respiratory treatments, and the case was rescheduled[243].
Surgical Apgar score: 9
Recommended.

Dr. Juan Fernando Velez Moreno, MD
Email: juanfvm@yahoo.com
Member of CTSnet.org, the Latin American Society for Cardiovascular and Thoracic Surgery.
Dr. Velez is very pleasant with excellent English. He is widely acknowledged within Bogota to have excellent surgical skills and was the previous Chief of Pediatric Cardiac Surgery at Cardioinfantil for eleven years before leaving to return to his home in Medellin, (where he worked at Clinica Medellin for four years). He is a University of Alabama at Birmingham pediatric cardiac surgery fellowship alumni. He currently works on a rotational basis with Dr. Pineros for pediatric cardiac surgery and Dr. Guerra for adult surgery. While Dr. Velez expresses frustration with the performance of Mederi, he remains hopeful that he will be able to implement necessary changes in the future. He is currently working with Boston Children's Hospital to improve pediatric cardiac services and has plans for improvements to

---

[243] This is entirely appropriate. Any sort of airway compromise, such as airway constriction as seen in asthma places the patient at increased risk for significant complications.

Mederi. He remains committed to remaining at Mederi to provide care for the underserved in Bogota.

This surgery program is *Not Recommended. Excessive postoperative mortality.*

Smaller cardiac surgery programs/ solo surgeon practices

Dr. Rafael Rodriguez, MD
Email: rafikiruge@gmail.com
Email sent; no reply received.
Member of CTSnet.org, the Latin American Society for Cardiovascular and Thoracic Surgery. Reported to work at the Universidad el Rosario.

Dr. Amador Burgoa, MD
Carrera 17 No 95 – 06
Bogota, Colombia
Tele: 616 8970
Email: amadorburgoa@cable.net.co
Emailed to request interview; no reply received. Member of CTSnet.org, the Latin American Society for Cardiovascular and Thoracic Surgery.
Dr. Burgoa operates at Clinica Fundadores in the Teusaquillo neighborhood.

Dr. Aminta Capasso, MD
Email: amintocapasso@cable.net.co
Emailed to request interview, no reply received.

Partial listing on CTSnet.org, member of the Latin American Society for Cardiovascular and Thoracic Surgery.
Dr. Capasso operates at Hospital de San Jose.

Dr. Nevio Rodriguez, MD
Dr. Nevio Rodriguez is the sole cardiac surgeon at Hospital Militar. He has been working at this facility for thirty years. He primarily performs bypass surgery, valve replacement and repair of the aorta in cases of aneurysm or dissection. Dr. Rodriguez is very kind and genteel but speaks only Spanish.
He currently performs about five cases per week/ 200 cases per year. He reports that the program at this facility is small as the military hospital in Medellin performs the majority of heart cases including transplant.
Dr. Rodriguez is not listed on CTSnet.org

Thoracic Surgery

In addition to the usual range of thoracic procedures performed in the United States, thoracic surgeons in Bogota frequently perform sympathectomies[244] as well as mediastinal surgeries for mediastinitis and other complications from open heart surgery[245]. Thoracic surgeons also perform specialized pediatric procedures such as thoracoscopic correction of sternal deformities such as pectus cavernosum.

In Colombia, there is currently only one thoracic surgery program, located at El Bosque, with primary residency training sites at Hospital Santa Clara and the National Cancer Institute.

Due to the limited number of thoracic surgeons in the Bogota area, many of the surgeons practice at several hospitals throughout the city, similar to Dr. Edgar Guitterez, who was profiled in the Hidden Gem Cartagena edition[246]. In many cases, this comes at considerable personal sacrifice, as there is a heavy burden of thoracic disease in the less glamorous public hospitals serving the

---

[244] Thoracoscopic sympathetomies are used to treat hyperhidrosis, Reynaud's disease and excessive palmar sweating. This procedure is becoming more popular in the United States.

[245] Since surgeons in the United States typically perform both cardiac and thoracic surgery, cardiac surgeons usually perform their own mediastinal revisions in cases of infection or poor wound healing after heart surgery.

[246] There are currently 52 thoracic surgeons in Colombia. However, despite this small number, they appear to be underutilized.

indigent populations in the southern part of the city, but much less financial compensation for their services[247].

Special Focus: Patient Education

Pre & Post-operative Surgical Optimization for Lung Surgery:or How to speed healing and reduce complications

As most of my patients from my native Virginia can attest; pre & post-operative surgical optimization is a critical component to a successful lung surgery. In most cases, lung surgery is performed on the very patients who are more likely to encounter pulmonary (lung) problems, either from underlying chronic diseases such as emphysema or asthma or from the nature of the surgery itself.[248]

During surgery the surgeon has to operate using something called "unilung ventilation." This means that while the surgeon is trying to get the tumor out – you, the patient, have to be able to tolerate using only one lung (so he can operate on the other.) Pre-surgical optimization is akin to training for a marathon; it's the process of enhancing a patient's wellness prior to undergoing a surgical procedure. For diabetics, this means controlling blood sugars prior to surgery to prevent and reduce the risk of infection. It also means obtaining current

---

[247] For a more detailed discussion of the life of a Bogota thoracic surgeon, please see *The Thoracic Surgeons: Bogota, Colombia*.

[248] Plainly speaking: the people, who need lung surgery the most, are the people with bad lungs which makes surgery itself more risky.

vaccinations (flu and pneumonia) six weeks prior to surgery, if possible[249]. For smokers, ideally it means stopping smoking 4 to 6 weeks prior to surgery[250]. It also means *Pulmonary Rehabilitation.*

Pulmonary Rehabilitation is a training program available at most hospitals and rehabilitation centers that maximizes and builds lung capacity. Numerous studies have shown the benefits of pre-surgical pulmonary rehabilitation programs for lung patients. Not only does pulmonary rehabilitation speed recovery, reduce the incidence of post-operative pneumonia[251], and reduce the need for supplemental oxygen, it also may determine the aggressiveness of your treatment altogether.

In very simple terms, when talking about lung cancer remember: "Better out than in." This means patients that are able to have surgical resection (surgical removal) of their lung cancers do better and live longer than patients who receive other forms of treatment such as chemotherapy or radiation.

If you are fortunate enough to have your lung cancer discovered at a point where it is possible to consider surgical excision – then you need to take the next step, so you are eligible for the best surgery possible. It is critical for you to enhance your lung function through a supervised walking and lung exercise program so the

---

[249] It is important to continue to receive regular immunizations for influenza (flu) and pneumonia after surgery.

[250] Even after a diagnosis of lung cancer, stopping smoking 4 to 6 weeks before surgery will promote healing and speed recovery. Long term, it reduces the risk of developing new cancers.

[251] Which can be fatal.

surgeon can take as much lung as needed. In patients with marginal lung function[252], the only option is for wedge resection of the tumor itself. This is a little pie slice taken out of the lung with the tumor in it. This is better than chemotherapy or radiation and is sometimes used with both – but it is not the best cancer operation available because there are often little, tiny, microscopic tumor cells left behind in the remaining lung tissue.

The best cancer operation is called a lobectomy where the entire lobe containing the tumor is removed. (People have five lobes, so your lung function needs to be good enough for you to breathe with only four[253]. This is the best chance to prevent a recurrence because all of the surrounding tissue where tumors spread by direct extension is removed (en bloc) as well. Doctors also take all the surrounding lymph nodes, where cancer usually spreads to first[254]. This is the best chance for five-year survival and, by definition, cure. But since doctors are taking more lung (a larger segment), patients need to have better lung function, and this is where a specialized exercise program called Pulmonary Rehabilitation comes in. In six weeks of dedicated pulmonary rehabilitation – many patients who initially would not qualify for lobectomy or for surgery at all – can improve their lung function to the point that surgery is possible.

---

[252] Lung function that permits only a small portion (or wedge section) to be removed.
[253] A gross measure of lung function is stair climbing; if you can climb three flights of stairs without stopping, you can probably tolerate a lobectomy.
[254] This is done for both further cancer staging and treatment.

Post-operatively, it is important to continue the principles of pulmonary rehab with rapid extubation (from the ventilator[255]), early ambulation (walking the hallways of the hospitals[256]) and frequent "pulmonary toileting" (i.e. coughing, deep breathing and incentive spirometry.) All of these things are important for surgery at any geographic location, but it is particularly important here in Bogota due to the increased altitude.

One last thing:

a. Make sure to have post-rehabilitation Pulmonary Function Testing (PFTs, or spirometry) to measure your improvement. Bring these results to your surgeon.

b. walk daily before surgery (training for a marathon, remember) bring home (and use religiously!) the incentive spirometer provided by rehab.

---

[255] This is often done at the conclusion of surgery in the operating room unless lung function is particularly poor or patient is unable to maintain adequate respiration without assistance.

[256] This is why chest tube drainage systems have handles. (So get up and walk!)

Dr. Leonardo Arrogoces, MD, MSc
Email: leonardoarrogoces@cable.net.co
Dr. Arrogoces reports that he no longer performs surgery and has not done so in several years. He currently works for the Ministry for Social Protection. He retains active membership in the Latin American Society for Cardiovascular and Thoracic Surgery, and his CTSnet.org listing.

Dr. Rodolfo Valentin Barrios Del Rio, MD
Edificio Horizonte Av. Calle 127 #20 – 78
Consultorio 715
Bogota, Colombia
Tele: 259 5500
Email: drbarriosdelrio@gmail.com
Dr. Barrios speaks some English.
He confirms that he was named after Rudolf Valentino. Dr. Barrios is originally from Cartagena and comes from a family of medical professionals. His father is a general surgeon, his mother is a surgical nurse and one of his two brothers is an anesthesiologist. Not on CTSnet.org, but reports membership in the Colombian Society of Pulmonology and Thoracic Surgery is pending. He is not a member of the Colombian Surgical Association because he feels the organization does not represent his interests. Dr. Barrios completed his thoracic surgery training at El Bosque and is a relatively new thoracic surgeon, though he has several years experience as a general surgeon. He currently works at Clinica Santa Clara with Dr. Stella Martinez and Dr. Andres Franco. He also works at

SaludCoop – Jorge Pineros Corpus campus, and the Reina Sofia clinic.

Currently, Dr. Barrios is working on publishing several case reports with Dr. Beltran. He is also researching the use of intrapulmonary chemotherapy and radiation for patients with metastatic lung lesions (non-lung primary cancers). These patients are being stratified into two groups: operative and non-operative. The patients who are unable to tolerate surgery receive a combination of chemotherapy and targeted radiation by percutaneous catheters.

The surgical arm undergoes a pulmonary metastasectomy with intra-operative radiofrequency ablation of cancer tissue.

This project is in the immediate stages with results not yet available for further scientific or medical publication. I was unable to observe surgery due to time and scheduling constraints.

Dr. Rafael Beltran, MD
Email: rbeltran@cancer.gov.co
Speaks Spanish primarily.

I was able to schedule an interview immediately after meeting Dr. Beltran in person at the monthly thoracic surgery meeting.

Dr. Beltran is originally from the northern coastal area of Colombia (Cartagena). He attended the University of Cartagena and spent his one year of mandatory rural service after medical school in a small coastal town[257]. He completed his general surgery training at Javieriana University and his Thoracic surgery training at El Bosque in the National Cancer Institute program. He has been operating for sixteen years.

Dr. Beltran is the Chief of Thoracic Surgery at the National Cancer Institute. He also operates at the University of the Americas, and Clinica de Marly. He enjoys the mix of cases that this provides. He has an avid interest in tracheal surgery and has published multiple articles on the subject, many in collaboration with Dr. Barrios[258]. During the interview he shares the details of several complex tracheal resections he recently performed. As the Chief of Thoracic Surgery for the largest cancer center in Colombia, Dr. Beltran also has extensive experience in the treatment of patients with rare and advanced cancers[259]. He also treats patients who develop complications from large surgical resections in outside facilities. He credits the development of a large, cohesive, multi-specialty surgical approach[260] to the high number of successes they have had with very complex surgeries requiring extensive reconstruction.

---

[257] After graduating from medical school, all physicians are required to spend six to twelve months providing care in an underserved area. Only six months are required for service in more volatile areas where the paramilitaries remain active.

[258] He and Dr. Barrios currently have an article on pancoast tumors pending publication.

[259] The more uncommon the cancer, or presentation – the more likely the patient is to be referred to Dr. Beltran.

[260] This means that prior to surgery, orthopedics, plastic surgery, thoracics along with pain management and diagnostics (radiology) collaborate to plan and proceed with these cases for the maximum benefit to the patient.

In addition to large open resections for gross disease, he also performs VATs procedures including single-port VATs and uses clamshell incisions as well as standard sternotomies to access mediastinal tumors, which reduces post-operative pain and has a more cosmetically pleasing appearance.

In his spare time, he enjoys using computers and technological gadgets, photography and spending time with his three sons and family. He also enjoys history and reading about world politics.

Dr. Miguel Ricardo Buitrago, MD
Calle 108 No 14B – 04
Bogota, Colombia
Tele: 214 0916 / 612 3873
Email: Buitrago77us@yahoo.com

Email sent requesting interview; received reply in a timely fashion. Dr. Buitrago speaks fluent English.

Dr. Buitrago attended medical school at Javieriana, and completed his general surgery residency there as well. He completed his thoracic surgery training at El Bosque. He continues to perform a limited amount of general surgery procedures, primarily at Hospital Simon Bolivar. He was performing an abdominal surgery when I arrived for the initial interview. He estimates general surgery accounts for less than 10% of his practice.

Dr. Bruitago is a member of the Colombian Surgical Association and the Colombian Association of Pulmonology and Thoracic Surgery, the Latin American

Society for Cardiovascular and Thoracic Surgery. He has a partial listing on CTSnet.org.

He currently works at the National Cancer Institute (Bogota) and is the joint deputy for the national welfare system. He was Director of the National Cancer Institute for eight years and remains an active board member. He also operates at Hospital Simon Bolivar, Clinica Shaio[261], Clinica Marly and Clinica Palermo. Currently, Dr. Buitrago is working to start a robotic thoracic surgery program using the DiVinci robot at Clinica Marly. He recently returned from robotic surgery training in the United States and reports that one of the premiere American thoracic (robotic) surgeons is coming to Bogota to help start the new program. Dr. Buitrago's major interests include robotic and hybrid procedures, thoracoscopic surgery, sympathectomies and treatment of pleural effusions.

He continues to have an interest in lung transplantation but does not feel that the programs in Bogota are competitive with the transplant surgery programs in Medellin. He has published several papers in thoracic surgery.

Despite my hesitation to observe further surgical procedures at Clinica Shaio, I observed several cases with Dr. Buitrago. Notably, the cases were blemish-free with continuous anesthesia monitoring and no hypotension or uncorrected hemodynamic instability. The attending

---

[261] In fact, Dr. Buitrago and his team performed the first lung transplant at Shiao Clinic in 1997, on a patient with emphysema. The patient received a double lung transplant.

anesthesiologist was Dr. Barrero, and he stayed in attendance to assist the anesthesia residents with double lumen tube placement and uni-lung ventilation during the cases. All standardized protocols followed, with no deviations from accepted practice guidelines.

During one case, Dr. Buitrago performed a thymectomy via a VATs procedure[262], utilizing several small 'port' incisions approximately 1 to 1.5 cm in length, which will speed recovery and reduce post-operative pain in comparison to the standard incisional technique. During the cases, Dr. Buitrago's experience and comfort level with the procedures was obvious, leading to uneventful cases without complications. On a separate visit, I observed Dr. Buitrago and his team perform a tumor resection on a teenaged patient at the National Cancer Institute, which is a teaching institution for thoracic surgery residents. This particular case was particularly complex as the tumor was adhering to the pericardium and other vital structures[263]. The tumor had also penetrated the chest wall, requiring painstaking removal, as well as chest wall reconstruction with prosthetic bone and muscle flap creation[264]. Prior to the case, films and case history were reviewed, compression devices applied, and invasive hemodynamic

---

[262] Versus a traditional sternotomy incision which is a midline incision through the breastplate.

[263] This increases the complexity of a lung tumor case by approximately ten-fold, as pericardial and great vessel involvement can lead to hemodynamic instability and cardiac instability during the case.

[264] The tumor had invaded a portion of the ribs which had to be removed en bloc.

monitoring lines placed[265]. All preoperative protocols followed: (timeout, antibiotics, etc.).

During this case the thoracic fellow took an active role as lead surgeon under the continuous assistance of Dr. Buitrago, who performed the more delicate aspects of the surgery[266]. During the case there was continuous anesthesia and hemodynamic monitoring, with no significant hemodynamic changes. No intra-operative complications.

Surgical Apgar scores: 9
Apgar score for extensive chest wall resection case: 7
Highly recommended. Experienced, talented surgeon.

Dr. Alvaro Casallas Gomez, MD, FACS
Avenida 9 No 117 – 20
Bogota, Colombia
Tele: 215 2300
Email: acasallasg@unal.edu.co

Speaks English. Responded readily to my request for an interview. His office is located in the medical building adjacent to Santa Fe de Bogota, where he shares an office with his wife, who is a neonatologist. Dr. Casallas attended and trained at National University, where he is now an associate professor of surgery. He performed his post-doctoral training in thoracic surgery at the University of South California and received his board certification in 1984. He also has a master's degree in Hospital

---

[265] This is important due to the reasons mentioned in footnote 196.
[266] See footnote number 204 for a discussion of levels of resident participation

Administration. He is the former Director of Hospital San Juan de Dios.

He is a member of the Colombian Surgical Association and a Fellow in the American College of Surgeons.

He currently operates in several facilities including Colsanitas group of facilities, Medisanitas facilities, Santa Fe de Bogota, Clinica de Marly and Clinica del Country. He operates at the Clinica de Marly most often, but retains operating privileges and operates at the other facilities according to patient and referring physician preference.

He was a close colleague to the now deceased Dr. De La Hoz, and reported that together they published several articles on myasthenia gravis, which is one of his main interests.

He is currently writing a book about thoracic trauma as part of his professorship at National University. He reports that thoracic trauma was a natural topic for him because of his expensive experience in this area, especially during the twenty years he worked and taught at Hospital San Juan de Dios[267]. He also sees his book as the perfect canvas to share his life experiences from that time. He reports that his primary research, over twenty years ago, was the basis for the change in practice from tube thoracostomy to decortications for the treatment of empyema in Colombia[268]. He also reports that he was instrumental in changing the protocols to perform mini-thoracotomies with coastal resection on critically ill

---

[267]This Bogota landmark closed in 1999.
[268]Research references and publication citations requested but never received.

patients versus the larger open thoracotomy[269]. Dr. Casallas states he originally became a surgeon because he likes the autonomy that the profession allows. He also likes to see outcomes of treatments[270].

Dr. Andres Franco, MD
Calle 108 No 14B – 04
Bogota, Colombia
Tele: 214 0916 / 612 3873
Email: donjuanandres2011@hotmail.com

I initially met Dr. Franco at Clinica Shaio, and exchanged contact information. Dr. Franco readily agreed to an interview.

Dr. Franco speaks fluent English.

Dr. Andres Franco is dually certified as both an ICU intensivist and a thoracic surgeon, and a busy one at that, working in both capacities at several facilities across the city. He currently works at two government facilities: Hospital Santa Clara and Hospital de Kennedy[271], as well as Clinica Shaio, Clinica Occidental and Fundacion Santa Fe de Bogota. His story is quite interesting; after completing medical school, and general surgical training, Dr. Franco worked in a rural part of the Colombian jungle

---

[269] Over fifteen years ago.

[270] This is a common theme among surgeons, and I share similar sentiments myself. Surgery allows us to see immediate results and benefits to our patients versus medical treatment or medications which may take months or years to show benefits.

[271] Hospital de Kennedy is located in southern Bogota, in a poorer part of the city.

with his wife[272] for a few years. He then returned to Bogota for additional medical training.

After completing his critical care medicine training at the University del Rosario, Dr. Franco embarked on his thoracic surgery training at El Bosque. This range of training serves to further his interests in postsurgical management of thoracic patients. He also enjoys pediatric thoracic surgery[273] and performing VATs procedures. Dr. Franco places a lot of emphasis on the doctor- patient relationship, and despite his busy schedule, actively strives to spend as much time as possible with his patients. He feels it is important for his patients to have his cellular phone number and to feel free to call him, if needed.

In his spare time he enjoys spending time with his wife, and infant son, participating in sports and traveling. He is currently preparing for his first triathlon.

Dr. Juan Carlos Garzon, MD
www.toracoscopica.com
Unidad Medica del Country
Cra 16 No. 82 – 95, Consultorio 907
Bogota, Colombia
Tele: 218 4897
Website with section in English.

---

[272] who is also a physician, Dr. Alexandra Gongora. She currently works at Clinica Shaio (Shaio Clinic) in the Intensive Care Unit.

[273] Dr. Franco primarily performs pediatric cases at Clinica Shaio, which has a better range of pediatric equipment that Hospital Santa Clara and some of the other facilities.

Emailed, then contacted via another surgeon. On my initial visit Dr. Garzon was at another hospital seeing patients but came to meet me at Cardioinfantil. After a brief interview, we scheduled a second visit for the following week to review cases, and visit the operating room, with a follow up interview for case review, and observation of patient rounds.

Dr. Garzon speaks excellent English.

Dr. Garzon operates at several facilities including Fundacion Cardioinfantil, Clinica Reina Sofia (Clinica Colsanitas), Clinica del Country, and Clinica Colombia (Colsanitas). Until recently, he was also working with Dr. Carlos Rodriguez at Hospital Militar Central. He is an active member of the Colombian Association of Pulmonology and Thoracic Surgery, and serves on the committee for thoracic surgery, member of the Latin American Society for Cardiovascular and Thoracic Surgery. Dr. Garzon completed his training in minimally invasive thoracoscopic surgery at the University of Hong Kong after completing his thoracic surgery specialty training here in Bogota.

Dr. Garzon is a former DJ, who now organizes on-going VATS (video assisted thoracoscopy) training throughout Colombia. In addition to pulmonary resections, pleurodesis, blebectomies and the usual range of lung procedures, sympathectomies and thoracic tumor excisions (thymomas, thyroids, etc), he reports occasional esophagectomies in the past[274].

---

[274]This surgery, usually performed for esophageal cancer is a high complexity condition (for a variety of reasons), and should only be

During surgeries Dr. Garzon performed the same incision closure techniques that are frequently employed by surgeons here in Colombia to minimize cosmetic disfigurement and scarring[275]. This added no additional surgical time and provides a distinct cosmetic advantage. All standardized protocols followed; with pre-operative review of cases, timeouts, proper patient positioning and intra-operative film reviews. Strict aseptic technique maintained, technically proficient. Patients remained hemodynamically stable throughout the cases.
Surgical Apgar scores : 8
Highly recommended. Gifted surgeon.

Dr. Luis Garcia – Herreros, MD
http://www.luisgarciaherrerosmd.com
Ave 9 No. 116 – 20
Consultorio 613
Bogota, Colombia
Tele: 215 0375
Email: lggarcia_herreros@hotmail.com
Dr. Garcia responded but declined an interview. Dr. Garcia – Herreros completed his thoracic surgery specialty training at the University El Bosque. He is currently the Chief of Surgery at Santa Fe de Bogota.

---

performed by a board certified thoracic surgeon, preferably in a high volume clinic. Minimum competency for this surgery is 12 cases per year.

[275] In comparison to common surgical practices in the United States.

Dr. Julio C. Granada Camacho, MD
Previously listed as a thoracic surgeon at now-defunct Santa Fe de Bogota webpage. No current address or information available on-line. Not listed on CTSnet.org.

Dr. Marco A. Hernandez, MD
Calle 38 No 8 -28
Bogota, Colombia
Tele: 232 – 7272
No internet listing found; no CTSnet listing. No listing with Colombian Surgical Association.

Dr. Andres E. Jimenez Quijano, MD
Email: jaejimenez@gmail.com
Emailed to request interview; replied in a timely fashion. Previously listed as a thoracic surgeon on a now-defunct Santa Fe de Bogota webpage, No CTSnet.org listing. Speaks some English.
Member of Colombian Surgical Association, Colombian Society of Pulmonary and Thoracic Surgery, American College of Chest Physicians.
Dr. Jimenez is young, 32 years old at the time of our interview. He graduated from Military University (Universitario Militar) in 2002. He completed his general surgery residency at the same facility. He completed his specialty training in 2008 at El Bosque. He then traveled to Barcelona for additional training in lung transplantation, which remains one of his avid interests along with the surgical treatment of malignancies.

He currently works at Hospital San Ignacio in addition to Santa Fe de Bogota, performing on average, 5 – 6 surgeries per week. He performs the whole range of thoracic procedures including sympathectomies, pulmonary resections, mediastinal procedures, and esophagectomies. In his spare time, he enjoys listening to rock music, playing golf and traveling.

In the operating room Dr. Jimenez is calm and relaxed. All pre-operative protocols, including time-out, pre-operative film review, and timely antibiotic administration, were performed. During patient repositioning the airway was secured and protected. During pre-operative preparations the blood pressure cuff gave low readings. After checking proper cuff functioning, an arterial line was immediately placed to verify these readings, which were shown to be erroneous[276]. The patient was hemodynamically stable throughout the case[277] with continuous anesthesia monitoring. Pneumatic compression devices were not used during this case, which was short in duration.

Surgical Apgar score: 8

Recommended. All protocols and procedures followed.

---

[276] An arterial line is an 'iv' catheter placed into an artery – often the radial artery at the wrist for more accurate hemodynamic monitoring. In this case, the actual blood pressure was consistently in the 120's – 140's, with the blood pressure cuff readings artificially low.

[277] Which is particularly notably as in this case, the patient had several significant co-morbidities including sub-optimally controlled atrial fibrillation, morbid obesity, diabetes, and a bleeding disorder with multiple antibodies (making blood compatibility matching difficult).

Dr. Mario Lopez Ordonez, MD
Email: marioandreslopez@gmail.com

Not on CTSnet.org. Speaks English well.

Dr. Lopez is a member of the Colombian Association of Pulmonology and Thoracic Surgery. Dr. Lopez currently works at Mederi, Clinica Santa Clara, and Clinica San Rafael. He became a general surgeon in 1994 and worked as a general surgeon until 1998 when he returned for additional hospital training as a thoracic surgeon at the National Cancer Institute. (This program was later recognized as part of the El Bosque program.) He was a professor of thoracic surgery at Militar hospital. In addition to working at three hospitals he also serves as a medical reviewer for a company investigating lawsuits. He has also written research papers on a trial performed for the treatment of malignant pleural effusions. Dr. Lopez has been investigating the utility of ambulatory drainage devices that would allow his patients to go home rather than remain hospitalized.

In the operating room Dr. Lopez is focused and deliberate. During the painstaking removal of a large, isolated[278] chondrosarcoma from the anterior chest, he carefully excised the tumor from around several very large blood vessels, ligating vessels imbedded in the tumor itself. Despite the highly vascular nature of the case, blood loss was minimal and well controlled. Despite operating in Mederi, which is an older facility, the operating rooms are large, clean, with modern equipment. Sterility was

---

[278]No evidence of metastasis, or other areas of disease in this patient.

maintained during the case, anti-embolism compression devices used, with appropriate antibiotic use, pre-operative beta blockage. The anesthesia team maintained a constant presence, and the patient remained hemodynamically stable at all times. Case films were hung for pre and intra-operative viewing. At the conclusion of tumor excision, Dr. Torres, of plastic surgery assumed the case to create a muscle flap and skin grafting to cover the excised area.

Surgical Apgar score: 8
Dr. Lopez is recommended.

Dr. Stella Isabel Martinez Jaramillo, MD
Calle 127 N 20 – 78
Consultorio 704
Bogota, Colombia
Tele: 679 1259
Email: simartinez@etb.net.co

Attempted to contact several times; first email address attempted bounced; alternative email delivered. Able to make initial contact using social media. Dr. Martinez is recommended by several colleagues.

Speaks English.

The initial interview was performed at Clinica Reina Sofia which is one of several facilities where Dr. Martinez works with subsequent interviews at Clinica Santa Clara. She also operates at Clinica del Country, and Clinica Santa Clara. Dr. Martinez attended Pontifical Xavierian University, completed general surgery residency at Pontifical Xavierian University, at SaludCoop Carolina.

Dr. Martinez completed thoracic surgery residency at El Bosque in 1994, with clinical coursework at the National Cancer Institute with Dr. Buitrago. Dr. Martinez has a wide variety of interests within thoracic surgery including bronchoscopy, tracheal surgery, VATs procedures, surgical treatment of malignancies, myasthenia gravis / thymectomy and prevention of respiratory complications in the ICU populations post-operatively. These interests are reflected in her extensive body of academic publications, primarily in Colombian and South American journals. She has also authored several chapters in a textbook published in Buenos Aires and presents frequently at conferences and academic events. She is a member of the Colombian Society of Pulmonology and Thoracic Surgery. She is also the co-Director of Mediastinal Atlas[279], a professional collaboration between Argentina and Colombia for the advancement of diagnosis and treatment of mediastinal disease. Dr. Martinez is the Director of the Thoracic Surgery residency program at Hospital Santa Clara and takes this responsibility seriously. She expects residents on her service to be prepared, engaged and dedicated to the study of her specialty.

For several years Dr. Martinez was the sole female thoracic surgeon in Colombia, which she takes in stride. Even while discussing past difficulties of obtaining thoracic surgery training in a male dominated profession where

---

[279] Dr. Juan Carlos Garzon Ramirez is also listed as one of the members of the editorial committee.

she was actively discouraged, she mentions several famous female thoracic surgeons, as well as the presence of another female surgeon here in Bogota, and an additional thoracic surgery resident.

Dr. Martinez has a reputation as a fair, but serious and strict, attending among surgical residents; I also found her to be kind and generous to her patients.

Prior to operating, cases and radiographs were reviewed, preoperative scrubs, time out procedures and other protocols followed. Sterility was maintained during cases. There was continuous anesthesia monitoring with no significant hemodynamic changes. Note: Cases were observed at Hospital Santa Clara, which is a teaching institute, with residents performing many of the surgical procedures, with Dr. Martinez, present, instructing and assisting at the operating room table[280].

Surgical Apgar scores : 8 - 9

Highly Recommended, very conscientious. For surgical tourism purposes, recommend treatment at Hospital Reina Sofia[281]*256.*

---

[280] This is standard procedure at many teaching facilities. However, there are levels of resident participating and attending assistance. In some cases, residents perform only opening and closing incisions, and the physician may be absent. In other cases the residents perform the majority of the surgery under the watchful guide of the experienced surgeon who is at the operating room table, scrubbed, and assisting in every aspect. If residents only had minor participation, such as retracting (holding tissue), participation was not noted.

[281] Reina Sofia is a nicer facility with more patient amenities than Hospital Santa Clara.

Dr. Camilo Osorio Barker, MD
http://www.camiloosorio.com
Centro de Especialistas en Cardioinfantil, Pisa 1
Bogota, Colombia
Tele: 861 55 55, Ext. 2605 (university)
667 2767 (cardioinfantil)
Email: consulta@camiloosorio.com

Speaks some English. Website in Spanish only.

Dr. Osorio replied quickly to an email request for interview. The initial interview was in Chia at the University of Sabana, where he is the Dean of Medicine[282]. Follow up interviews were performed at Cardioinfantil and the University hospital in Chia.

Dr. Osorio attended medical school and completed his general surgery residency at University Pontifica Boliveriana in Medellin, Colombia. He completed his thoracic surgery training at the Hospital Santa Creu and Santa Paul in Barcelona, Spain.

Dr. Osorio is a member of the Colombian Surgical Association, the Colombian Society of Pulmonology and Thoracic Surgery, and the Latin American Society for Thoracic disease (ALAT). He is also the President of the South American Society of Thoracic Surgery.

Dr. Osorio primarily specializes in sympathectomies for hyperhidrosis (or excessive sweating). He estimates that 90% of his cases are sympathectomies with the remainder being lung resections, lung biopsies and pleurodesis. Dr. Osorio also has several YouTube videos on explaining and

---

[282] Chia is a small town just north of Bogota.

demonstrating his thoracoscopic sympathectomies for patient information, in addition to an informational site on sympathectomies at[283]:

http://www.truedoctors.com/Hyperhidrosis-articles.htm. He currently operates at the University hospital in Chia, Cardioinfantil with Dr. Tellez and Dr. Garzon, and at another hospital in Medellin. He sees patients at the Medellin location three days per month. During rounds and consultations with patients, Dr. Osorio is thorough and personable. He takes time to explain procedures fully and to answer patients' questions. He also makes a point of calling patients several days before and after surgery to solicit additional questions or concerns. Several of the patients I saw with Dr. Osorio were referred by former patients.

In the operating room Dr. Osorio is precise and efficient. In less than fifteen minutes (per side) the sympathectomy procedure was completed. It actually takes longer to prepare the patient for surgery than the procedure itself. While I did not witness a formal "time-out" for both cases, Dr. Osorio walked through an informal time-out procedure that covered all of the elements except timely antibiotic administration[284]. I was able to verify the time

---

[283] This is a surgical tourism site, but the articles listed are of good information value. However, the statement that this procedure is "noninvasive" is false. While this surgery is 'minimally-invasive' by means of thoracoscopy it is still a surgical procedure, using general anesthesia, surgical incisions and entry into the chest cavity – all of which is, by definition, invasive.

[284] As part of the patient consent review process, Dr. Osorio reviewed the patient history and physical, procedure planned, site of procedure, and the

and type of antibiotic administered, but this information was not included in the surgical reports[285].
Surgical Apgar score: 9
Recommended; excellent surgical proficiency.

Dr. Francisco Palacio Nieto, MD, PhD
Email: Francisco_palacio2000@yahoo.com
Emailed to request interview, no reply.

Dr. Mauricio Pelaez Arango, MD
http://med.javeriana.edu.co/cirugia/introduccion_cirugia
Unidad Medica del Country
Cra 16 No. 82 – 95, Consultorio 907
Bogota, Colombia
Tele: 218 4897
Email: mapelaez@yahoo.com
Dr. Pelaez is a previous associate professor of surgery at Javeriana University Medical School, and the Chief of Surgery at San Ignacio. He completed six months of his thoracic surgery fellowship at the University of Pennsylvania, with the remainder completed at the University El Bosque. He is currently completing a vascular surgery fellowship, and will be a board certified vascular surgeon this November (2011)[286]261. He is completing his endovascular training in Spain.

---

other required elements of the 'time-out' process with exceptions noted above

[285]Information verified asking during the procedure, and visually identifying medication bottles on the IV infusion set.

[286]Due to his extensive surgical experience as a general and thoracic surgeon, the training program was shortened from two years to one.

Not currently a member of CTSnet.org.

He is a member of the Colombian Surgical Association and former coordinator of the Committee on Thoracic Surgery (2007 – 2009). There are multiple research citations available from his previous employment in academics. He reports he left academics because he wanted to focus more of his time on surgery and his patients. Dr. Pelaez currently operates at the Hospital San Ignacio, Cardioinfantil (as a vascular surgery resident) and Clinica del Country. He still performs occasional general surgery cases such as cholecystectomies and appendectomies, and takes occasional general surgery call. He also performs pediatric thoracic surgery, in addition to the standard range of adult thoracic surgery. He particularly enjoys tracheal surgery, pneumonectomies, treating mediastinal tumors and lung cancer. As part of his fledging vascular practice, he will be performing a range of peripheral vascular procedures such as varicose vein removal, peripheral bypass and endovascular surgery.

In his rare spare time, he enjoys tennis and working on his small farm in La Calera.

Dr. Pelaez did not initially respond to written and informal requests to visit the operating room. He replied (two months later) with a surgery date which was after the date of my departure. However, I was able to observe Dr. Palaez in the operating room on a follow-up visit to Bogota. I observed Dr. Palaez in the operating room at Clinica del Country, and during his rounds as both a fellow (vascular surgery at Cardioinfantil) and at Clinica del Country.

In the operating room, all procedures and protocols were followed with proper patient positioning, identification, and an administration of medications. Excellent anesthesia coverage during the case with no fluxuation in vital signs or alterations in hemodynamic status.
Surgical Apgar Score: 10, skilled surgeon

Dr. Jairo Ramirez Cabrera, MD, FACS
Av 9 No 117 – 20
Consultorio 818
Bogota, Colombia
Tele: 215 0959
Email: jairo.ramirez@ama.com.co
Emailed to request interview with prompt reply.
Speaks German, English and Spanish.
Not listed as a member of the Colombian Society of Vascular Surgery. Membership as a fellow in the American College of Surgeons verified.
Completed medical school and general surgery residency at Javieriana University. He completed additional training in vascular and thoracic surgery at the Ludwig Maxmillian University of Munich in Germany, 1986.
Dr. Ramirez reports that he no longer performs thoracic surgery. He states that he primarily performs peripheral vascular surgery, and the majority of his vascular cases are for the treatment of venous disease such as varicosities and venous stasis ulcerations. He reports that surgeries for arterial disease are rare in his practice because the majority of his patients present late with areas of ischemia and necrosis already in evidence.

Dr. Nelson Ricardo Renteria, MD
http://www.ricardorenteriamd.com
Centro Vascular del Country
Carrera 18 No 79 – 40
Consultorio 201
Bogota, Colombia
Tele: 611 3447

Carrera 23 No 45 C – 31
Consultorio 204 Norte
Bogota, Colombia
Tele: 287 0448
Email: toraxau@yahoo.com.au

Email directed at the email address provided at the Colombian Society for Vascular Surgeons bounced. Dr. Renteria is a vascular and thoracic surgeon. He attended Universitario el Rosario for medical school. He completed his general surgery residency was at Hospital Militar and Clinica San Rafael. He then completed both his vascular and thoracic training at El Bosque, as well as a thoracic surgery fellowship in esophageal surgery under Dr. F Griffith Pearson at the National Cancer Institute in Toronto, Canada. He received additional training in France for port-a-cath placement using ultrasound guidance. He performs approximately 300 long term intravenous access procedures a year.

He is a member of the Colombian Society of Vascular Surgeons and the Colombian Society of Pulmonolgy and Thoracic Surgeons. He was previously listed as a consulting physician for a telemedicine group on-line at http://www.telemedicinavascular.com but is no longer active in this practice. He is the former Chief of General Surgery at El Rosario and has a large patient population composed of Red Cross employees.

He currently operates at Kennedy Hospital in South Bogota, which is a hospital specializing in thoracic and vascular trauma. He also operates at Clinica Palermo and maintains an active thoracic and vascular practice. He estimates that 50% of his patients are thoracic patients. As part of his vascular practice, he employs a radiologist, Dr. Cecilia Villasante, to perform non-invasive diagnostic procedures, as well as a physical therapist for lymphadema treatment and a wound and ostomy nurse for management of venous stasis ulcers. Forty percent of his practice is dedicated to the management of venous disease with the remaining ten percent of his practice composed of arterial disease management and port-a-cath placement for chemotherapy.

Dr. Renteria is the only thoracic surgeon currently performing esophagectomies in Bogota. He performs approximately 20 to 25 esophagectomies a year, using a combination of Ivor-Lewis, transhiatal and tranthoracic approaches. He also performs some uniportal thoracoscopic surgery (SITS).

During the first case, a thoracic surgery case requiring general anesthesia and uni-lung ventilation, at Hospital de Kennedy, the quality of anesthesia was poor, despite continuous monitoring by both the anesthesia resident and the attending anesthesiologist. The patient experienced significant hypotension for the majority of the case that was only marginally addressed. The heart rate was also unchecked, resulting in tachycardia for the duration of the case. The preoperative antibiotic was given late, and no anti-embolic devices were employed. No pre-operative time-out was witnessed, but the surgeon reviewed the film and case history with staff and myself prior to the case. Sterility was maintained throughout the case.

The quality of the anesthesia resulted in a very low Apgar score which is exceedingly unfortunate, as Dr. Renteria proved to be an excellent surgeon on this, and subsequent cases, observed at another facility.

I observed several vascular cases at the Compensar ambulatory surgery center. The anesthesia at this facility was excellent, a combination of regional blocks and conscious sedation administered by Dr. Alcides Polania with continuous anesthesia monitoring. All patients were hemodynamically stable during the cases and reported excellent post-operative pain control. Cases proceeded according to all standardized protocols and procedural guidelines with no intra-operative complications.

Surgical Apgar Score: Hospital de Kennedy: 3
Surgical Apgar score: Compensar : 8
Recommended for procedures outside of Hospital de Kennedy only due to poor anesthesia. Surgeon technically proficient.

Dr. Carlos Rodriguez, MD
Email: charlier09@hotmail.com

Contact information provided by Dr. Jimenez, emailed for interview. Confirmed appointment in person during chance meeting at SaludCoop. Despite confirming our appointment, I waited an additional twenty minutes for Dr. Rodriguez to arrive with three residents in tow. Dr. Rodriguez then immediately informed me that he had only a few minutes to spare, despite having no further cases that day. Dr. Rodriguez speaks only Spanish. He answered my questions but was somewhat brusque and impatient. He immediately handed me off to his residents when I requested to round the wards to see his current patients[287]. I was not allowed to view the intensive care unit, the operating room suites or the recovery room where one of his patients was recovering after surgery that morning.

He did tell me that Hospital Militar, where we met, had established a thoracic surgery program 14 years prior, and now serves as the primary training program for thoracic surgery in Colombia[288]. Dr. Rodriguez worked for Clinica Santa Clara for eight years prior to working at SaludCoop and Hospital Militar.

Dr. Rodriguez did not respond to my request to observe surgery[289].

---

[287] In-patients were limited to three patients with pleural effusions and one patient undergoing evaluation to determine whether he was a candidate for surgical resection for a primary lung tumor. One of the pleural effusion patients had undergone thoracoscopy with talc pleurodesis.

[288] This information was not confirmed by other thoracic surgeons.

[289] which is disappointing as he has a local reputation as an excellent surgeon, particularly for trauma, and open cases.

Dr. Luis Jaime Tellez Rodriguez, MD
http://www.jaimetellezmd.com/
Calle 163A No. 13B – 60
Centro de Especialistas, 2nd Floor
Fundacion Cardioinfantil IC de Bogota
Bogota, Colombia
Tele: 667 - 2767
Email: torax@jaimetellezmd.com or
ltellez@cardioinfantil.org

Emailed to request interview; Dr. Tellez responded quickly to schedule. Dr. Tellez is multi-lingual and speaks English, German and Portuguese in addition to his native Spanish. He is not listed on the CTSnet.org registry. Additional profile information available at www.susmedicos.com/torax including several articles on thoracic topics authored by Dr. Tellez, (in Spanish). Dr. Tellez is the former coordinator for the South American thoracic surgery conference (conference XIII), and presenter. He is a member of the Colombian Association of Pulmonology and Thoracic Surgery, head of Thoracic Surgery committee, member of the Colombian Surgical Association. Dr. Tellez is the Chief of Thoracic Surgery at Cardioinfantil and works with Dr. Garzon and Dr. Osorio[290] at Cardioinfantil, Clinica Colombia and Reina Sofia.

Dr. Tellez comes from a family of physicians, including his grandfather, his father and his son. He is a professor of

---

[290] Dr. Osorio's involvement is more limited in this capacity; he does not see patients at Clinica Reina Sofia or Clinica Colombia. Please see his individual profile.

thoracic surgery[291] and has worked as a thoracic surgeon for thirteen years. Prior to that, he worked as a general surgeon. In 1998, Dr. Tellez completed his two year thoracic surgery specialty training at Santa Casa de Misericordia in Porto Alegre, Brazil.
Currently, he performs VATs (video-assisted thoracoscopic surgery), medistinoscopies/ mediastinotomies, and additional mediastinal procedures for the treatment of mediastinitis after bypass surgery. The majority of his cases are bronchogenic carcinomas. Dr. Tellez is planning to start a lung transplant surgery program in the future.
In his spare time he can be found jogging around Bogota, playing golf or spending time with his wife and two sons. Dr. Tellez never responded to my requests to observe him in the operating room[292].

Dr. Luis Fernando Rueda Marulanda, MD
Calle 91 No 19 C – 55
Bogota, Colombia
Tele: 618 5034
Email: luisfermd@hotmail.com
Contacted to schedule interview. Dr. Rueda now practices in Barranquilla, a coastal city in Colombia.

---

[291] Universidad de Rosario and Universidad de la Sabana.
[292] Both informal and written requests.

Dr. Hernando Russi Campos
Email: hrussi@javieriana.edu.co

Emails bounced; reported as "over quota." After multiple attempts, finally contacted Dr. Russi via another surgeon. Dr. Russi speaks Spanish only.

Dr. Russi attended National University medical school and completed his general surgery residency at the same facility. He completed his thoracic surgery training at El Bosque in 1979.

Dr. Russi is the senior thoracic surgeon at Hospital San Ignacio and is a Professor of Thoracic Surgery at that facility.

In the past he has held similar teaching positions at Javieriana, El Bosque, and Universitario San Martin.

References for Additional Information
Tourism Information

Colombia Minister of Tourism
www.colombia.travel
The Colombia tourism division offers an official guide to tourism in Colombia along with a well-designed, attractive multi-media website with additional information for travelers and tourists. Both available in English.

Discover Colombia:
http://www.discovercolombia.com
Maps and general information about Colombia.

Visitemos a Bogota: y sus polos de atraccion turistica
(book.)
This book is bilingual tourist guide to Bogota and local attractions. It also includes a detailed city map. This book is available locally in Bogota bookstores. Ask for "una guia de cuidad de Bogota con ingles." It is also available from the publisher:
Cosmoguias Ltda.
Calle 70 N 28 – 28
Bogota, Colombia
PBX: 630 0130
cosmoguias@gmail.com
cosmoguias@yahoo.com
Omar Bechara, the founder of this company also produces many of the beautiful scenic postcards of the city.

References for additional information about surgical specialties, medical information:

American College of Surgeons
www.fasc.org
633 N. Saint Clair Street
Chicago, Il 60611 – 3211
Tele: 312 202 5000
Email: postmaster@fasc.org

The American College of Surgeons designates members as 'Fellows" also seen as "FACS" after the surgeons' name. Fellowship is entirely voluntary and requires completion of specific criteria such as board-certification in a specific surgical specialty, with a thorough review of the surgeons' educational qualifications, credentials and professional standing. The American College of Surgeons maintains a patient education section which includes information on surgical procedures. The American College of Surgeons also maintains a searchable database for designated fellows. To find a member of the American College of surgeons or to verify credentials as a fellow:
http://www.facs.org/patienteducation/patientresources/surgery/acsmember.html
There are 29 fellows listed in the Bogota area.

The Cardiothoracic Surgery Network (CTSnet)
http://www.ctsnet.org
CTSnet is not a regulatory board or organization but it is the largest, most comprehensive on-line source for information on cardiothoracic surgery. CTSnet.org has

affiliations with organizations and surgical societies in over 48 countries, and most surgeons maintain a profile listing their background, training, current practice and interests. Individual surgeon contact information is also provided. While this information is primarily intended for physicians, residents and medical students, it is available to the public for review but requires guest sign-in to access information.

Colombian Association for Obesity and Bariatric Surgery
A complete list of members by city is maintained at: http://www.acocib.com/miembros.html

Colombian Society of Orthopedic Surgeons
http://www.sccot.org.co/
Website in Spanish with member registry.

Colombian Society of Plastic Surgery
http://www.cirugiaplastica.org.co/
Website in Spanish only. Visitors are able to verify surgeons' education, training and licensure.

Colombian Surgical Association
www.ascolcirugia.org
The Colombian Surgical Association maintains a list of practicing members, including email addresses. The list is arranged by city, in alphabetical order. This list can be viewed at: www.ascolcirugia.org/asociadosActivos.htm

International Organization for Standardization (ISO)
ISO standards are voluntary recommendations, policies and procedures adopted by facilities as regulations for their internal practices. The ISO is a large scale organization which provides standards of practice for multiple industries including engineering, manufacturing, medical devices and healthcare. Standards for the healthcare industry include regulations for aseptic/ sterile processing of equipment, medical device guidelines, privacy requirement for healthcare information (similar to our HIPPA laws).
For more information: http://www.iso.org

Joint Commission International (JCI)
Joint Commission International is the international arm of Joint Commission (formerly JHACO), which is the regulatory organization responsible for hospital accreditation. Joint Commission sets hospital standards and protocols governing a wide variety of areas including post-surgical infections, and surgical complications, nosocomial (hospital acquired) illnesses such as MRSA (methacillin resistant staphylococcus aureus), medication administration, and pharmacy standards.
Joint Commission regulations and recommendations are considered the most stringent currently available, and JCI performs on-site inspections and performance appraisals. Individual hospital scores are available to the public for scrutiny.
Major criticisms of JCI include the enforceability of protocols and standards (participation is not mandatory in

many areas), and advanced notice of hospital inspections. For more information:
http://www.jointcommissioninternational.org/

The Surgical Apgar Score

One of the most important parts and, in fact, one of the principles of this project, is the operating room visit. This is the part of the evaluation that patients cannot judge for themselves and is rarely judged by others; yet the surgical procedure itself plays a monumental role in determining outcomes.

The Surgical Apgar score, devised by Gawande et. al in 2007, determined that independent of pre-operative patient risk classification, that three intra-operative risk factors played the biggest role in determining the development of major complications up to 30 days post-operatively.

These three risk factors were: estimated blood loss (EBL), lowest heart rate and lowest mean arterial pressure (MAP)[293].

Using this information, Gawande et. al. devised a 10 point tool which assigns a score to intra-operative management. From this score we are able to estimate the risk of developing complications, and the risk varies dramatically with the score.

For example, with a score of 9 or 10 (the highest), the risk of complications is about 5 percent. However, this risk

---

[293] Mean arterial blood pressure is an average derived from both the systolic and diastolic values.

increases to 56% with a score of 4 or less[294]. In patients that did develop post-operative complications, Regenborgen & Gawande demonstrated in a large scale study, those patients with a score of 2 or less were twenty times more likely to die than patients with a score of 9 or 10.

This tool has been well tested and validated in several large studies involving thousands of patients making it a valid measurement of performance and an essential tool for objective intra-operative assessment[295].

One of the reasons this scale is so powerful, is that it is able to determine risk independent of patient factors such as advanced age and underlying co-morbidities. In fact, by using this scale as part of intra-operative assessment, surgeons and anesthesiologists can reduce their patients' risk of complications dramatically.

During application of this scale to cases witnessed, the main area of point loss was consistently heart rate control. This meant that an otherwise excellent surgery, with a

---

[294]Regenbogen, S. E., Lancaster, R. T., Lipsitz, S. R., Greenberg, C. C., Hutter, M. M., & A. A. Gawande. (2008). Does the surgical Apgar score measure intra-operative performance. Ann. Surg. 2008, Aug; 248(2): 320 – 328.

[295]Regenbogen, S.E., Bordeianou, L., Hutter, M. M., & A. A. Gawande (2010). The intra-operative surgical Apgar score predicts post-discharge complications after colon and rectal resection. Surgery. 2010 Sep, 148(3):559-66.

Ohlsson, H. & Winso, O. (2011). Assessment of the surgical Apgar score in a Swedish setting. Acta Anaesthesiol. Scand. 2011 Mar 21, epub.

Haynes, A. B., Regenbogen, S. E., Weiser, T. G., Lipsitz, S. R., Dzieken, G., Berry, W. R. & A. A. Gawande. (2011). surgical outcome measurement for a global patient population: validation of the surgical Apgar score in 8 countries. Surgery. 2011, epub Jan 8.

lowest heart rate of 86 lost all four possible points for the category.

This tool is also an excellent assessment tool for surgeons to apply to see where necessary improvements should be made.

Government Agencies for American Travelers

US Department of State
Standard government issued warnings and disclaimers with specific mention of potential complications of elective surgery and unlicensed pharmaceuticals intended for enhancing sexual performance.
http://www.travel.state.gov/travel/cispatw/cis/cis1090.html#medical

American Embassy Information
American Citizen Services is a department of the US Embassy which can assist Americans travelling in Colombia in emergency situations, such as the illness, serious injury or death. Citizen services are also available for emergency assistance in cases of violent crime, or arrest.

Emergency Contact Information
In Colombia, call: (1) 315-0811 – staffed 24 hours a day. Email: ACSBogota@state.gov (place "emergency" in subject line). Please note email only checked between normal business hours, 9 am – 5 pm, Monday thru Friday, non holidays.

Embassy at Bogota:
http://bogota.usembassy.gov/

The Embassy's American Citizen Services office is located at Calle 24 Bis No. 48-50 in Bogotá, Colombia. Calle 24 Bis is a small street near the intersection of Carrera 50 and Avenida Esperanza, with Calle 26 as another major nearby road.

Look for the American Citizen Services sign at the gate. You will also see a long line of Colombian residents outside, at a separate entrance, applying for visas. The American resident entrance is on the opposite side of the Embassy compound from the entrance for visa applicants. Limited hours: 8:30am –
12 noon, Monday – Thurs.

The Embassy maintains a list of health care providers (physicians and dentists) for emergencies.
http://bogota.usembassy.gov/root/pdfs/medservices.pdf
Joseph Santos, PA-C, a physician assistant at the Embassy in Bogota confirmed the criteria for inclusion in the list of preferred providers. Criteria include: validation of credentials, easy accessibility and availability of written follow up reports. The vetting process for inclusion on the list is primarily credential based, with no in-person interviews or case review. Potential applications submit an application, a resume and references from former patients for consideration.

Appendix A: Emergency Information / Urgencias

Name (Nombre)_____

Home Address / Direccion_____
_____
_____

Local Address / Direccion en Bogota_____
_____
_____

Telephone number / numero de telefono_____
Surgeon / cirujano_____
Date of medical procedure/ Fecha de operacion_____
Medical Procedure/ Que operacion? _____
_____

Location of procedure (nombre de clinica)

_____

Additional Medical History:
[ ] Diabetes
[ ] High blood pressure /presion alta
[ ] Heart disease /problemas cardiacos
[ ] Lung disease/ problemas pulmones
[ ] Bleeding disorder /tendecias a sangrar
[ ] HIV (SIDA)
[ ] Hx of smoking / fumas tabaco

Other medical Conditions / Otras problemas_____
_____
_____

Allergies: Alergias _____
_____

Medications/ Medicinas
1._____
2._____
3._____
4._____
5._____
6._____
7._____

Are you taking blood thinners? [ ] yes [ ] no Mark if applicable:
[ ] aspirin / aspirina [ ] "Coumadin"/ warfarin,
[ ] "Plavix"/ clopidogrel [ ] "Effient"/ prasugrel
[ ] "Aggrenox"/ aspirin/extended release dipyridamole)
[ ] "Pradaxa" / dabigatran
[ ] Other _____
Date last taken / Fecha de medicinas_____

Appendix B

Helpful Spanish Phrases

While many of the healthcare providers in Colombia either speak English or have translators readily available, the average Colombian citizen may or may not speak English. It is also considered good manners to at least attempt to speak in Spanish when conversing. Even if you have little to no knowledge of Spanish, your efforts will earn the goodwill of many Colombians.

In general, most Colombians are very friendly and helpful and will be happy to assist you in your efforts to communicate.

Keys to pronunciation:

H at the beginning of words is often silent. Double 'L' is a y sound as is "yes"

Greetings/ Getting Around

Good day……………..Buenos dias. (primarily used in the mornings)
Good afternoon………Buenas tardes. (used from noon to late evening)
Good night...…………..Buenas noches. (utilized as an evening greeting or bedtime).
Hello…………………...¡Hola!
How is it going?……... ..¿Que tal?
How are you?...............¿Como estas?
My name is …………. ..Me llamo....
I am fine………………..Estoy bien.
Please ……….. …….. ...Por favor.

Thank you................Gracias.
You're welcome.........De nada or por nada (literally means, "it's nothing".)
Pleased to meet you.....Mucho gusto...
Pardon me.....................Perdon.
Do you speak English? .. ¿Habla ingles?
I do not speak Spanish. ...Yo no hablo espanol.
I do not understand..........No entiendo.
I need help ....Necesito ayuda.
I'm sorry.......................Lo siento.
I'm lost..........................Estoy perdido.
Can you help me?................¿Puede ayudarme?
Where is the bathroom? ...¿Donde esta el bano?
Can you speak slowly?.......Puede hablar mas despacio.

Medical / Health

Symptoms
I feel sick .... Me siento enfermo.
I have pain ....Tengo dolor.
I have nausea .... Tengo nausea or tengo mareo
I have vomited.........He vomitado or vomite.
I am vomiting..........Yo estoy vomitando.
I have diarrhea ....Tengo diarrea.
I have a fever ....Tengo fiebre.

Needs/ Physical Comforts

I need medicine for pain ....Necesito medicamento para el dolor.
I need medicine for nausea ... . Necesito medicamento para la nausea.

I want to see the doctor ....Quiero ver al doctor.
I need a doctor......................Necessito un medico.
I want to go to the bathroom....Quiero ir al bano.
I am hungry......................... Tengo hambre.
I am thirsty............................Tengo sed.
I need a drink of water............Necesito agua para tomar.
Call a doctor! ....¡Llama a un medico!

Medical Questions

Where is the nearest hospital? .¿Donde esta el hospital mas cercano?
Are you the doctor?.................... ¿Es usted el doctor?

Other questions

What time...?..............................¿A qué hora...?
Where?.......................................¿Dónde?
From where?..............................¿De dónde?
Which direction?........................¿Por dónde?
To where?.................................. ¿A dónde?
How?...¿Cómo?
Which one/-s?............................ ¿Cuál/-es?
When?...¿Cuándo?
How much?.................................¿Cuánto/-a?
How many?.................................¿Cuántos/-as?
What?... ¿Qué?
For what reason?........................¿Para qué?
Why?... ¿Por qué?
Who? ....¿Quién/-es?
To whom?...................................¿A quién?
For whom?..................................¿Para quién?
Whose?.......................................¿De quién/-es?

278

Appendix C – Limited Drug Guide

This information is provided for emergency use. While all attempts have been made to provide the most accurate information possible, there is no way to verify the medications in all circumstances due to the lack of pharmaceutical regulations in this destination. This section should be used in combination to conversations with your medical providers to ensure accuracy and safety.

Many pharmacies in Bogota are privately owned and operated by non-pharmacy trained personnel who are not qualified to prescribe or provide medical and medication advice. Please remember this when purchasing medications.

Key
Generic name in italics
(Trade name in parenthesis)
Brief description of medication.
Colombian brand names in Bold

Acetaminophen - (Tylenol)
Analgesic (pain reliever), antipyretic (fever reducer). Use caution with this medication as it is often combined with other medications in numerous other products including cough syrups and narcotic pain relievers. Acute and chronic over ingestion of acetaminophen is a major cause of liver failure.

Acetaminofen La Santé® - (La Santé), Acetaminofén MK, Acetaminofen (Pentacoop), Adorem (California), Ametrex (Anglopharma), Dolex (GlaxoSmithKline), Kenox (Caribe), Winadol (Grupo Farma)

Albuterol - (Proventil)
Inhaler, tablet, or syrup used as a bronchodilator to help with shortness of breath in asthma or chronic obstructive pulmonary disease. May cause tachycardia (fast heartbeats).
Airmax (Chalver), Ciplabutol IDM (Biotoscana), Ciplabutol (Biotoscana), Salbutamol Ecar, Salbutamol Genfar (Genfar), Salbutamol (Merck), Salbutamol MK, Salbutamol (Pentacoop), Servitamol (Novartis), Ventilan (GlaxoSmithKline)

alendronate – (Fosamax)
biphosphanate drug used in the treatment / prevention of osteoporosis.
Alendronato Genfar, Alendranato La Sante, Alendronato MK, Alendronato, Armol, Bifemelan, Eucalen, Fixopan, Fosamax, Lokar, Neobon, Osficar, Ostex.

aliskiren – (Tekturna)
anti-hypertensive direct renin inhibitor.
No information available.

amiodarone – (Cordarone, Nexterone, Pacerone)
Potent anti-arrhythmic used for life-threatening arrhythmias. Like all anti-arrhythmics, amiodarone has potentially serious side effects and should not be taken long-term unless under the direction of a cardiologist.
Amiodarone La Sante, Amiodarona Merck, Amiodarone MK, Amiorit, Cordarone, Daronal.

amlodipine – (Norvasc)
calcium channel blocker, used in the treatment of hypertension, heart disease.
Amdipin, Amlodipino Genfar, Amlodipino La Sante, Amlodipino MK, Amlodipino, Amlosyn, Amlotens, Euroran, Norvas, Vasten

amlodipine + benazepril – (Lotrel)
combination medication containing calcium channel blocker, and an ace inhibitor. Used to treat hypertension and heart disease. No information available.

apipiprazole – (Abilify, Abilify Discmelt)
psychiatric medication. Atypical anti-psychotic and antidepressant.
Abilify (Colombian drug name the same)

Aspirin - (Aspirin)
analgesic, anti-inflammatory, antipyretic, and antithrombotic effects.
Acido Acetil Salicilico AZ, Alka Seltzer (Bayer), ASA MK, Asawin (Sanofi-Aventis), Cardioaspirina (Bayer), Ecotrin (GlaxoSmithKline)

aspirin + dipyramidazole – (Aggrenox)
Antiplatelet agent, for prevention of stroke.
No information available.

atenolol – (Tenormin)
A beta-blocker that lowers heart rate and blood pressure. Used in the treatment of heart disease and as a secondary blood pressure medication. Also an important pre-operative medication to lower the risk of heart –related peri-operative complications. Similar to metoprolol.
Atenolol MK, Plenacor, Tenormin.

atorvastatin – (Lipitor)
statin drug used to lower cholesterol, treat heart and vascular disease.
Atorlip, Atorsyn, Atorvastatina Genfar, Atorvastina La Sante, Atorvastatina MK, Atorvastina, Atorarol, Axo, Biostatina, Farmalip, Glustar, Lipitor, Lowlipen, Nivecol, Pakadel

benazepril – (Lotensin)
ace-inhibitor. Used to treat heart disease including congestive heart disease, hypertension. Also used to prevent and treat chronic renal failure.
No information available.

budesonide – (Entocort EC, Pulmicort, Rhinocort)
Steroid (glucocorticoid) used to treat asthma, chronic inflammatory bowel disease, and rhinitis.
B-cort, Ciplabude, Inflammide, Miflonide, Prehistam, Pulmicort, Rhinocort Aqua, Timalar, Timat

bupropion – (Wellbutrin, Aplenzin, Budeprion SR/XL, Bupropion XL, Buproban, Wellbutrin SR/XL, Zyban)
psychiatric medication. Anti-depressant. Also used to assist smoking cessation efforts. Multiple formulations including sustained, and extended release. Do not combine with nicotine patch- may cause malignant hypertension.
Odranal, Wellbutrin

candesartan – (Atacand, Blopress, Amias, Ratacand)
angiotension receptor blocker (ARB) used to treat hypertension and heart disease.
Candesartan Genfar

carvedilol – (Coreg, Coreg CR)
A beta-blocker similar to metoprolol tartrate that lowers heart rate and blood pressure. Used in the treatment of heart disease including congestive heart disease, and as a

secondary blood pressure medication . Also an important pre-operative medication to lower the risk of heart – related peri-operative complications.
Carvedil, Coryol, Dilatrend, Vasodyl.

celecoxib – (Celebrex)
non-steroidal anti-inflammatory (NSAID), commonly used for arthritis. No safe dosage has been established for patients after a recent myocardial infarction (heart attack.) Patients should check with their cardiologists before taking any NSAID after a heart attack.
Celebrex, Celecoxib Genfar, Celecoxib La Sante, Celecoxib, Cicloxx-2, Dilox, Flonar, Lexfin

cetirizine - (All day Allergy, Zyrtec, Cirrus)
anti-histamine used to treat allergies, hay fever.
Acidrine, Alercet, Alerviden, Cetirax, Cetirizina Genfar, Cetirizina La Sante, Cetirizina, Cetirrinol, Cetrine, Levoc, Optiser, Zyrfar, Zyrtec

clonidine – (Catapres, Catapres TTD, Duraclon)
Potent antihypertensive available in multiple forms including transdermal patches and epidural infusions. Epidural infusions used to treat refractory cancer pain. Multiple off-label uses.
Catapresan.

clopidogrel bisulfate - (Plavix, Iscover)
anti-platelet agent, used for patients with recent stents, cardiac or vascular disease. *It is critical that you inform*

all of your physicians that you are taking this medication. Do not abruptly discontinue this medication without informing your physician.
Algilis, Atelit, Ateplax, Clopidogrel La Sante, Clopidogrel MK, Clopidogrel, Clopivas, Flusan, Iscover, Plavix, Terotrom, Tisten

codeine – (Codeine)
Pain reliever, cough suppressant (caution: may be habit forming).
Codeina

dabigatran etexilate mesylate (Pradaxa)
anti-coagulant (blood thinner) used for stroke prevention, atrial fibrillation. *It is critical that you inform all of your physicians that you are taking this medication.* **Widely available in Bogota, under the trade name of Pradaxa but note that dosage may be different.**

digoxin – (Digitek, Digoxin, Lanoxicaps, Lanoxin)
medication used for treatment of heart disease including congestive heart failure (CHF), atrial fibrillation.
Digoxina

diltiazem – (Cardizem, Cartia XT, Dilacor XR, Dilt-CD, DiltiaXT, Diltzac, Taztia XT, Tiamate, Tiazac)
Calcium channel blocker, similar to verapamil; used to treat heart disease including angina, hypertension and atrial fibrillation.

diltiazem - continued
Corazem, Diltiasyn, Diltiazem Genfar, Diltiazem La Sante, Diltiazem, Tilazem, Umezar.

dolasetron – (Anzemet)
central acting anti-nausea, anti-emetic similar to ondansetron.
Anzemet

donepezil – (Aricept, Aricept OPD)
used in the treatment of Alzheimer's type dementias.
Alzit, Eranz

doxazosin – (Cardura)
alpha adrenergic receptor blocker used for hypertension, benign prostate hypertrophy. Similar to prazosin and terazosin.
Carduran, Dalgen, Doxazosina La Sante, Doxazosina Merck.

dronedarone – (Multaq)
Newer formulation of amiodarone, used for cardiac arrhythmias. Recent blackbox warning issued by the FDA.
Multaq Sanofi, No other information available.

duloxetine – (Cymbalta)
psychiatric medication. Anti-depressant, anti-anxiety.
Cymbalta

enalapril – (Enalaprilat, Vasotec)
Ace-inhibitor used to treat heart disease, hypertension and diabetic nephropathy; similar to lisinopril.
Biocronil, Enalapril, Enalapril Best, Enalapril Ecar, Enalapril Genfar , Enalapril la sante, Enalapril MK , Enetil, Giloten, Renitec, Tesoren, Unipril.

enalapril + felodipine – (Lexxel)
Combination of ace inhibitor and calcium channel blocker. felodipine is similar to amlodipine.
No information available.

enoxaparin – (Lovenox)
anti-coagulant, used in the treatment and prevention of blood clots.
Clexane

erythropoietin/ epoetin alfa – (Procrit, Eprex, Epogen)
medication used to stimulate the formation of red blood cells.
Epoyet

escitalopram – (Lexapro)
psychiatric medication, anti-depressant.
Dexapron, Lexapro

esomeprazole – (Nexium)
proton pump inhibitor used for acid reflux disease.
Cronopep, Esomeprazol Genfar, Esomeprazol La Sante, Esomeprazol MK, Esomezol, Esoprax, Esoz, Nedox, Nexium

exenatide – (Byetta)
Incretin mimetic, used to treat diabetes.
No information available.

ezetimibe – (Zetia)
Nonstatin, cholesterol lowering medication.
Ezetrol, Zetia

ezetimibe + simvastatin – (Vytorin)
combination cholesterol medication containing a statin (simvastatin) and another cholesterol lowering agent. No information available.

famotidine - (Pepcid)
antiacid, treatment of gastroesophageal reflux disease, indigestion.
Famotidina

felodipine – (Plendil)
Calcium channel blocker similar to amlodipine.
No information available.

fenofibrate – (Tricor, Trilipix, Lipofen, Lofibra, Antera, Triglide)
Fibrate medication used to lower cholesterol and decrease insulin resistance. Often used in combination with statins and other anti-lipidemic medications for control of hyperlipidemia.
Normolip

Fluoxetine - (Prozac)
Antidepressant.
Ansilan (Biogen), Fluoxetina Genfar, Fluoxetina La Santé, Fluoxetina MK, Fluoxetina (Pentacoop), Moltoben (Bussié), Pragmaten (Novamed), Prozac (Lilly)

fluconazole – (Diflucan)
Multi-purpose anti-fungal agent available in multiple forms. Used to treat wide range of fungal infections from vaginal candiasis to fungal infections in the bloodstream (fungemia) and internal organs. As with any antibiotic/anti-infective, repeat exposure or use leads to organism resistance, rendering the medication ineffective.
Baten, Aplaflucon, Diflucan, Farzul, Fluconazol La santé, Fluconazol MK, Fumex, Fuzol Pauly, Nobzol, Tavor.

fluticasone + salmeterol - (Advair)
respiratory medications for treatment of asthma and COPD. May be used in combination products or individually.
Flumar, Seretide

fondaparinux – (Arixtra)
anti-coagulant, used in the treatment and prevention of blood clots.
Arixtra

furosemide – (Lasix)
Diuretic
Furosemida Genfar, Furosemida La Sante, Furosemida MK

glimepiride – (Amaryl)
Sulfonyurea, oral antidiabetic agent, one of two classes of drugs used for oral treatment of diabetes according to current evidence based practice guidelines.
Amaryl, Glimepiride La Sante, Glimepiride MK, Glimerid, Gliride.

heparin - (Heparin, Hemochron, HepFlush)
Anticoagulant (high risk blood thinner). Important: should not be used without proper medical supervision. Usually used exclusively in hospitals; information provided here for patient reference.
Heparina Sodica (Comercial Médica), Lioton (Biotoscana)

hydrochlorothiazide – (Microzide)
Diuretic used for multiple purposes including congestive heart failure and hypertension.
Hidroclorotiazida Genfar, Hidroclorotiazida La Santé, Hidroclorotiazida MK, Hidroclorotiazida (Pentacoop)

hydralazine – (Apresoline)
vasodilator used for hypertension, and congestive heart failure.
Hidralazine Clorhidrato

hydralazine + isorbide dinitrate – (Bidil)
Combination medication for the treatment of heart failure.
No information available.

hydrocodone – (Lortab, Lorcet (formulation only comes as a combination product with Acetaminophen or Ibuprofen)
Pain reliever, cough suppressant (Caution: may be habit forming).
Hydrocodona

ibuprofen – (Motrin, Advil, Midol, Nuprin, Samson-8)
Non-steroidal anti-inflammatory medication. (NSAID).
Used for arthritis, post-operative pain, musculoskeletal pain. Not for chronic or long-term use.
Advil, Ainex, Apiron, Back Pain, Calmidol, Dol, Febrifen, Fenpic, Ibupiretas, Ibuprofeno, Mejoral, Motrin, Smadol, Trosifen

insulin determir – (Levemir)
a non-peaking, continuous acting basal insulin.
Levemir

insulin glargine analog – (Lantus)
a non-peaking, continuous acting basal insulin.
Lantus

irbesartan – (Avapro)
angiotension receptor blocker, used in the treatment of hypertension, and heart disease (same class of drug as valsartan).
No information available.

ketorolac – (Toradol)
Analgesic, anti-inflammatory (should not be used longer than 5 days).
Ketorolaco, Toradol

lamotrigine – (Lamictal)
anti-convulsant, also used as mood stabilizer. Multiple formulations including chewable, disintegrating tablets.
Lamictal

lansoprazole – (Prevacid)
proton pump inhibitor, same drug class/ family as esomaprazole. Multiple formulations.
Lacopen, Lanproton, Lansopep, Lansoprzol Genfar, Lansoprzol La Sante, Lansoprazol MK, Lansoprazol, Lanximed, Ogastro, Refluyet, Trogas

lisinopril – (Prinivil, Zestril)
ace inhibitor used for treatment of heart disease, hypertension and diabetic nephropathy.
Lispril, Tensyn

lisinopril + hydrochlorothiazide – (Prinzide, Zestoretic)
ace inhibitor combined with a diuretic. Similar formulation: enalapril + hydrochlorothiazide, brand name: Vasoretic.
No information available.

loratadine – (Alavert, Claritin, Clear-Atadine, Tavist ND,)
anti-histamine. Used for treatment of seasonal allergies.
Clarityne, Efectine, Histabloq, Loracert, Loramine, Loratidina Best, Loratidina Genfar, Loratidine La Sante, Loratidine MK, Loratidina, Valket

losartan – (Cozaar, Hyzaar)
angiotension receptor blocker, used in the treatment of hypertension, and heart disease (same class of drug as valsartan.)
Aralo X, Arapres, Cozaar, Losartan Genfar, Losartan La Sante, Losartan MK, Satoren, Tensartan

memantine – (Namenda)
For treatment of Alzheimer's dementia, or vascular dementia.
Akatinol, Eutebrol.

metformin – (glucophage)
oral anti-glycemic. Also part of several new combination medications. First line agent approved and validated internationally for treatment of diabetes, polycystic ovarian syndrome. Multiple off-label indications.
Dimefor, Glucophage, Metformin MK, Metsulina.

metoprolol – (Toprol XL, Lopressor)
A beta-blocker that lowers heart rate and blood pressure. Used in the treatment of heart disease, and as a secondary blood pressure medication. Also an important pre-operative medication to lower the risk of heart –related peri-operative complications. Several formulations including metoprolol tartrate and metoprolol succinate with different dosage schedules.
Beloc, Betaloc, Betaloc Zok, Betaprol, Lopresor, Metoprolol La Sante, Metoprolol Merck, Metoprolol MK, Metoprolol Tartrato, Metoprolol.

modafinil – (Attenace, Provigil)
psychostimulant used for narcolepsy and daytime sleepiness.
No information available.

montelukast – (Singulair)
Respiratory medication used for COPD, asthma.
Blow, Cerrokast, Leukotren, Lukast, Montelukast, Montelukast La Sante, Profilax, Singulair, Xalar.

naproxen – (Aflaxen, Aleve, Anaprox, Mediproxen, Naprelan, Naprosyn)
non-steroidal anit-inflammatory (NSAID) used to treat pain, arthritis.
Apronax, Colfem, Naprox, Naproxen, Naproxeno Genfar, Naproxeno La Sante, Naproxeno MK, Naproxeno sodico MK.

nitroglycerin – (Collegis, Deponit, Mini-tran, Nitrek, Nitro-Bid, Nitro-Dur, Nitro-Time, Nitrodisc, Nitrogard, Nitrol, Nitroligual, NitroMist, Nitroquick, Nitrostat, Nitrotab, Sustachron ER, Transdermal-NTG, Tridil)
Potent vasodilator used to treat heart disease; angina, coronary artery disease.
Nitroglycerina.

olanzapine – (Zyprexa, Zyprexa Relrevv, Zyprexa Zydis)
psychiatric medication, anti-psychotic. Multiple formulations, and off-label uses.
Dozic, Frenial, Olazap, Prolanz, Zyprexa.

olmesartan – (Benicar)
angiotensin receptor blocker (ARB) used to treat heart disease, hypertension. Similar to valsartan.
No information available.

omeprazole – (Prilosec)
Proton pump inhibitor (PPI) similar to pantoprazole, used to treat acid reflux.
Gastrosef, Losec mups, Melcornar, Meprox, Omeprax, Omeprazol Genfar, Omeprazol La Sante, Omeprazol MK, Omeprazole, Orazol, Peptidin, Tarzol, Ulcepar, Ulzone.

ondansetron – (Zofran)
anti-emetic for treatment of nausea and vomiting.
Modificial, Oncoemet, Ondansetron, Zofran Zydis, Zofran.

oxycodone – (As a combination product in Percocet or alone in Oxycontin).
Potent pain reliever (Caution: May be habit forming).
Oxycodona

paliperidone – (Invega)
Atypical anti-psychotic, treatment of schizoaffective disorder or schizophrenia.
Paliperidona, Invega

pantoprazole – (Protonix, Pantozol, Pantoloc)
proton pump inhibitor, same drug class/family as esomeprazole.
Segregan, Ugarpan

paroxetine – (Paxil, Paxil CR, Pexeva)
psychiatric medication. Anti-depressant, anti-anxiety. Also used to treat obsessive compulsive disorder and panic disorder.
Moxetin, Paxan, Seroxat.

pioglitazone – (Actos)
glycemic agent used for treatment of hyperglycemia, diabetes.
Glucemin

prasugrel – (Effient)
Anti-platelet agent approved for use in patients with coronary stents to prevent acute stent thrombosis. *Similar to clopidogrel; always inform your doctor if you are taking this medication.*
No information available.

pravastatin sodium - (Pravachol)
statin medication used to lower cholesterol.
Pravacol, Pravalip, Pravastatina, Pravyl.

pregabalin – (Lyrica)
anti-convulsant, for partial seizures. Also used for anxiety disorders, and fibromyalgia.
Lyrica

promethazine – (Phenergan)
Allergic conditions, anti nausea and vomiting, motion sickness, pre or postoperative analgesia/hypnotic adjunct, sedation (usually along with analgesic). Most commonly utilized for nausea or vomiting.
Prometazina

quetiapine - (Seroquel, Seroquel XR)
psychiatric medication, anti-psychotic.
Seroquel

rabeprazole – (AcipHex, Pariet)
proton pump inhibitor, same drug class/ family as esomaprazole. **Pariet**

raloxifene – (Evista)
treatment of osteoporosis and certain types of breast cancers.
Evista

ranitidine - (Zantac)
antiacid, treatment of gastroesophageal reflux disease, indigestion.
ranitidine

ramipril - (Altace)
ace-inhibitor. Used to treat heart disease including congestive heart disease, hypertension and chronic renal failure.
Tritace

risperidone – (Risperdal)
psychiatric medication, anti-psychotic.
Risofren, Risperdal

ropinirole – (Requip, Ropark, Adartrel)
Dopamine agonist used to treat Parkinson's disease, and restless legs. Requires dose titration.
No information available.

rosiglitazone – (Avandia)
glycemic agent used for treatment of hyperglycemia, diabetes.
Avandia

rosuvastatin – (Crestor)
a newer generation statin medication used to lower cholesterol.
Crestor

sertraline – (Zoloft)
psychiatric medication, anti-depressant.
Sertraline, Zoloft.

simvastatin – (Zocor)
statin drug used to lower cholesterol.
Simplaqor, Simvastin, Simvastina, Simvastina Genfar, Simvastina Merck, Simvastina MK, Zerocoler.

sildenafil citrate – (Viagra, Revatio)
used for erectile dysfunction and pulmonary arterial hypertension, and high- altitude pulmonary edema (off-label use).
Ejertol, Elebra, Erilin, Eroxim, Per-Lui, Sex-Men, Sildenafil Genfar, Sildenafil La Sante, Sildenafil Masticable, Sildenafil MK, Sildenofilo Colmed, Sildenofilo, Tranky, Viagra.

sitagliptin – (Januvia)
Anti-diabetic (for type II diabetes)
Januvia

sumatriptan – (Imatrex, Sumavel)
Anti-migraine medication. Newer combination medication (Treximet) is combination of sumatriptan and naproxen sodium.
Imigran, Migragesin, Sitran, Sumatriptan Genfar.

tadalafil citrate – (Cialis)
similar to sidenafil but with a longer (36 hour) effective period. For erectile dysfunction and treatment of pulmonary hypertension.
Cialis

tamsulosin – (Flomax, Flomaxtra, Urimax)
For treatment of benign prostatic hypertrophy.
Omnic, Proslosin, Secotex, Tamsulon.

telmisartan – (Micardis)
angiotension receptor blocker, used in the treatment of hypertension, and heart disease (same class of drug as valsartan.)
Micardis.

tiotropium – (Spiriva)
bronchodilator used for treatment of COPD.
Spiriva, Tiamar.

tolterodine – (Detrol)
Treatment of overactive bladder.
Detrusitol

topiramate – (Topamax, Topiragen)
anti-convulsant, alternative treatment for migraines.
Topamac

tramadol – (Ultram)
For moderate to severe pain, may have addiction potential, and can cause withdrawal symptoms if abused. For short term use of ten days or less. Schedule VI, along with all other medications requiring a prescription in the United States. Available in intravenous form in Colombia for in-patient use.
Tramol

trazodone – (Desyrel)
Antidepressant, may also be used as a sleep agent.
Trazodona

valproate, valproic acid, valproate semisodium –
(Depakote, Depakote ER, Depakene, Depacon, Stavzor)
anti-convulsant, mood stabilizer used for treatment of epilepsy, bipolar disorder, migraines and schizophrenia.
Acido Valproico Merck, Atemperator, Depakene, Ferbin, Valcote, Valprosid, Valsup.

valacyclovir – (Valtrex)
antiviral used to treat herpes (multiple forms) and other viral outbreaks.
Vadiral, Valcyclor, Valtrex.

valsartan – (Diovan)
argiotension receptor blocker, used in the treatment of hypertension, and heart disease.
Valsaprex, Valsartan Genfar, Valsartan MK, Valtan.

vardenafil – (Levitra, Vivanza)
similar to other PDE5 inhibitors such as sildenafil and tadalafil. Used for erectile dysfunction.
Levitra

verapamil – (Calan, Covera-HS, Isoptin, Veralan)
Calcium channel blocker available in multiple forms, including an ophthalmic solution. Used to treat glaucoma, angina, hypertension, arrhythmias and left ventricular hypertrophy.
Isoptin, Verapamilo, Verapamilo Best, Verapamilo Ecar, Verapamilo Genfar, Verapamilo La Sante, Verapamilo MK, Veratad.

venlafaxine – (Effexor, Effexor ER)
psychiatric medication, anti-depressant.
Efexor XR, Venlax.

warfarin – (Coumadin)
Anticoagulant (blood thinner). Notify your physician if you are taking this medication.
Coumadin (Britol-Myers Squibb)

zolpidem – (Ambien, Edluar, Zolpimist)
used to treat insomnia once sleep disordered breathing (obstructive sleep apnea, etc.) has been ruled out.
Dormeben, Solpirem, Somnil, Stilnox, Zimor, Zolpidem Genfar. Zolpidem La Sante, Zolpidem MK.

About the Authors

K. Eckland

My Story and My Mission
In my case, it began without warning; I had just published the first Hidden Gem guidebook, and was working in the Virgin Islands when I first become ill, and this progressively worsened until I presented to a local physician. After an emergency admission to the hospital and a series of tests, including one fateful CT scan, my life changed suddenly. While the doctors at the small island facility were able to relieve my immediate medical

problems, they lacked the resources to further diagnose or treat the underlying condition. I was advised to seek off-island care. After my previous visit to Colombia, I had no hesitation or questions about where to seek care. I immediately contacted some of the people I had previously interviewed, and arranged to return to Colombia. I had already planned to research and write a book about Bogota and had started the preliminary research when I became ill; now I had a new sense of urgency. Fortunately, the situation turned out to be less drastic than previously believed, but it remains life altering.

With this in mind I hope that this book helps others find peace of mind and good surgical care in their time of need.

K. Eckland, ACNP-BC, MSN, RN is an acute care nurse practitioner in cardiothoracic surgery. As a nurse and patient advocate, she feels passionately about patient education, making informed choices and knowing your options. She is relentless in her pursuit of truth and transparency in medicine and patient safety.

Albert Klein & his wife, Lauren

Albert Klein, PharmD is a Bogota native, now living and working as a hospital-based clinical pharmacist in North Carolina. He shares Kristin's enthusiasm and commitment to excellence in healthcare practice.
This is their second conjoined effort in a series of books exploring surgical tourism.

Made in the USA
Charleston, SC
18 September 2011